RESONANCE

www.get-known.co.uk

CONTENTS

WHO THIS
BOOK IS FOR

Welcome, reader, to a journey into the world of video content creation and the route to unleashing your brand's potential with video. I'm excited to share my knowledge of online video with you, arming you with (in my view) the most powerful weapon in a marketer's arsenal.

Creating video content for a business used to be a 'nice to have' and was low down on the marketing priority list – after branding, website, social media and the laundry list of other 'must haves'. But the tide has changed dramatically in recent years, driven by a consumer demand for online video content. All of us, the public, have embraced this new technology in our daily lives, from watching TV online to sharing videos with friends over social media. And as the popularity of online video has soared, the marketing world has learnt to take advantage of this trend.

Forward-thinking marketers are now making online video a cornerstone of their marketing strategy. They are using it to lift their brand above the competition and to communicate on a much more meaningful level with their customers. **The right video, used in the right way, can do more for your business than virtually any other marketing**

asset. Video is a hugely versatile medium that can be used to educate customers about your products, promote trust, encourage sales, generate buzz to put your business in the spotlight, and ultimately build up your customer's love for your brand. Marketers who embrace video can get better results from their marketing efforts and shout louder, longer and with more impact than their competitors.

I've written this book for anyone who wants their brand to resonate with an audience, and who wants to know the best way to do that: with video.

This book is for you if:

▶ You know video has great potential but you haven't managed to leverage it

▶ You've tried to get results with video but have never quite hit the mark (or worse, have gone over budget and wasted resources) and you're desperate to get the next project right

▶ You're overwhelmed by a lack of knowledge and experience in using video, so you are fearful of getting it wrong and making yourself look bad

▶ You're yet to find the right video partner – someone you can trust who really 'gets' what you are trying to say

▶ You want a marketing tool that can give you an advantage over your peers.

If you are a marketer looking to grow your brand, and you want video to be part of your strategy, then you're in the right place. Whether your brand is a peppy start-up trying to disrupt a sector, or an industry leader defending its position – and regardless of your sector, geography or target market – this book will help you unlock the power of video marketing. And if you are a professional at a digital marketing, PR or other creative agency looking to bring video into your client projects, this book will help you to integrate video in the right way, so you can get better results from your work.

This isn't a technical handbook for videographers or editors, and I won't be delving into 'this camera versus that camera' or 'this filming technique versus another'. If you are a video content creator looking to up your skills, there are books more suited to that. But if you want to learn how to get video right from idea to strategy, so that video becomes the one thing that ensures your brand and message cut through the ever-increasing noise and land firmly with your audience, then this book is for you.

PS: When you unleash your brand's potential with video, it's going to make you personally look really good too, and who doesn't want that?

THIS BOOK WILL...

This book will enable you to create video content that actually resonates with your customers. It's that resonance that will make them fall in love with your brand. And you can turn that love into sales.

Attempting to create video for your brand can be a really daunting process. Because video is quite technical, it's easy to get bamboozled by the jargon being used by suppliers, and it's hard to know how to allocate resources, what creative approach to take and even how to leverage your video effectively. The outcome of a video project often falls on your shoulders, with other stakeholders holding you to account for its success or failure. That's a lot of pressure to be under, and I've seen how it can create worry, stress and sleepless nights. I've had them myself at times.

I've worked with dozens of brand marketers over the years, and the one thing I've learnt is that our job as video supplier isn't just to deliver great video; it's also about helping our clients to make the right decisions, communicate those decisions effectively, and track the outcome of their campaigns so they can prove the value of their video project to their team. This book is designed to make things a lot easier for you, so your future video projects are fun and stress free while still delivering the outcome you were aiming for.

In this book, I'm going to walk you through my simple five-step method for creating resonance with your customers through video so you can unleash your brand's potential. We'll start with tying your video project to tangible business goals, and then I'll help you to come up with the right idea for your video, refine the story you are telling about your business, and project manage the production process so you get the best quality video for your budget. I'll even walk you through the best ways to leverage your videos to drive measurable results for your business. Along the way, I'm going to also share the common pitfalls and mistakes to avoid during your video project, together with some of my top tips for getting things right.

By the end of this book, you will be able to assemble a foolproof briefing document that will act as a roadmap for your video project and enable you to master this medium. Ultimately, I want you to be able to create resonance with your customers through video content that they enjoy and which adds value to their lives, so they join your tribe as brand evangelists.

By the way, you may be thinking 'hold on a second, if this guy thinks video is so great then why the hell has he chosen to write a book instead of making videos?' Well, I wouldn't be much of a video evangelist if I didn't practise what I preach. So, as you go through the book, you can also access a series of videos where I provide some additional tips to help you to unleash your brand's potential with video.

MEET
GEORGE HUGHES

As you can probably tell, I get a little overexcited about video. But it's hard not to get excited when I truly believe it is the one tactic that can give your brand the greatest edge. For over 25 years, I've been making films. From shooting my own home movies as a teenager, via 14 years in the TV industry producing and directing prime time series for most of the major broadcasters, to founding my company Small Films and working with start-ups and household name brands alike, helping them share their stories with the world.

I love the power of the moving image and its ability to capture people's imagination. The technology of video, combined with quality storytelling, is a hugely powerful tool for entertaining, educating and selling to your customers. I've made literally hundreds of hours of broadcast television, refining my storytelling skills for almost two decades. In that time I learnt the components of a good story, and I use that knowledge to help our clients spread the word about their products and services.

I love to see the impact we can create with a successful video project, whether it's growing a company from scratch to a seven-figure business or helping a market leader to reposition their brand image. As a self-confessed video game addict, I love to use the term 'levelling up'. And just as the video game characters who increase their skills get better gear and improve their level, I've always tried to do the same in my own life.

Throughout my TV career, I was always looking to level up – developing directing skills, finding out how to cast the best contributors, learning how to interview subjects better or understanding which camera kit got the best shots. Having worked on some highly successful series with millions of viewers, and other ones that flopped, I'd always wanted to know what ingredients made for the best TV shows and what made the worst.

Why was it that *Inside the Factory*, a show I worked on for BBC2, went on to multiple series, while *Leepu and Pitbull* on the History Channel was never recommissioned? The latter had a huge, multimillion-pound budget, great cast members and a compelling premise – 'car mechanics turn people's cheap, beat-up cars into supercars' – and yet it didn't get great ratings. Whereas *Inside the Factory* was a simple series with a modest budget, taking viewers behind the scenes of how our favourite foods were made. And it became one of the most popular BBC shows.

It was never an exact science, but I always noticed the hallmarks of a great series in the making and I began to get a feel for which would work, and which wouldn't. The one thing I always observed was that if the show didn't resonate with the audience, then it didn't matter how big your budget was, or how much drama or how big an explosion you put in, people just wouldn't watch it. That moment of resonance was absolutely paramount to a series being successful.

When I began my journey into branded video content, I wanted to continue levelling up my own knowledge as well as the skills, knowledge and experience of the team. From humble beginnings shooting a promo video for a local clay pigeon shooting company, I was determined to keep levelling up until we'd have the opportunity to work with recognised brands, where I knew we could bring the most value. So I spent a huge amount of time analysing and picking apart both our own work and other well-known campaigns, looking for the key components that made them successful. I realised that at the heart of it all was that same element I'd seen in TV shows: if the video didn't resonate with its audience, it wouldn't be successful. Creating resonance was absolutely fundamental. And I discovered that there are some critical elements of a video campaign that can ensure your video resonates with your audience and has the best chance of success. It's those discoveries that I want to share with you in this book.

I also discovered one other thing. It turns out there is, in fact, a secret ingredient that is the one common contributing factor to videos going viral, and virality is the holy grail for any video content creator. If you get to the end of this book, and you've paid attention, then you should spot a single theme emerging that will give you the answer to how to make your videos go viral. If you don't spot it, then email me to ask that all-important question: 'How do I make my videos go viral?' **george.hughes@smallfilms.com**

VIDEO CAN UNLEASH YOUR BRAND'S POTENTIAL

WE LIVE IN ONE OF THE MOST EXCITING TIMES IN HUMAN HISTORY

In the last 10 years, advances in technology have accelerated at an exponential rate. Ours is the time of artificial intelligence, advanced robotics and genetics. We've got robots that can walk on two feet, electric driverless cars, drones, space stations and multi-use rockets. We have augmented reality, blockchain, contactless payment and 3D printing. The list goes on.

The internet has also advanced rapidly. It's virtually unrecognisable from the days of Facebook founder Mark Zuckerberg sitting in his dorm room in 2004, working out how to create a website that he could use to rank the girls in his college on a 'hot or not' meter.[1] Today, Facebook has 2.4 billion users and the ability to topple governments and create new presidents.[2] Social media has now become an integral part of day-to-day life for many of us, and Generation Z (those born after 1997)[3] haven't known life without it. Today, most of us are online, doing everything from ordering groceries to buying clothes, from reading the news to chatting with friends… or even researching how the hell to write a book about video marketing! In 2019, we spent an average of three hours and 15 minutes online in the UK every day.[4] That figure always blows my mind but, when I think about it, it makes perfect sense.

At the heart of this massive shift is a device that most of us can't live without: the smartphone. A massive 78% of people own one in the UK,[5] which is no surprise given all the amazing ways it enriches our lives. We take for granted our ability to reference the entire encyclopedia of the world at the push of a button; listen to any piece of music ever composed or read any book ever written; communicate with anyone, any time through calls, messages and emails; communicate in any language we want using a real-time translator; download apps to assist our daily lives; and even make friends with thousands of people on different conti-

casting station in our pocket barely makes us bat an eyelash. We capture every single moment of our children's lives on film because we have an HD camcorder on our phone that's instantly available at a moment's notice. And if you want to get some super-slow motion shots of your kid on the swing, that's also possible, even though just 15 years ago, the only cameras that could shoot in super-slow motion cost about £100,000. You can even create your own YouTube channel about anything you want, from 'how to do woodwork' to 'my thoughts about life'. Oh, and you can monetise that with advertising and become a multimillionaire. Our ability to harness video has had an incredible effect on our daily lives in recent years and, with the advances currently being made in augmented reality, we're only seeing the start of it. You can watch a series of videos I recorded about this subject by following this link:

www.resonancebook.co.uk/videos

VIDEO OFFERS A GOLDEN OPPORTUNITY FOR MARKETERS

There are now a phenomenal number of tactics a marketer can deploy when trying to communicate with their customers, and there are countless marketing technologies available to us: from SEO to Google Ads, experiential campaigns to email marketing. Just 10 years ago, there were around 150 marketing technologies on the market; today, that number is closer to 8,000.[10] Knowing where to invest your budget, time and energy can be an absolute minefield, as well as a huge suck on resources. Yet video marketing has quietly powered through as a solid, reliable and highly effective marketing tactic. As a result, it is the fastest growing advertising medium and a whopping one-third of global online display advertising budgets are now spent on video.[11] So if you aren't riding that wave yet, you should be.

For marketers, the trend for video content creation and consumption presents a rare opportunity to reach our customers and advertise to them using our own video content. When they are watching videos about sourdough baking techniques on YouTube, we can be there. When they are reading the latest news or looking at the latest celebrity gossip, we can be there. Shopping sites, film streaming sites, online magazines, instant messaging, smartphone apps, email... the list goes on. So, whether you decide to run adverts on Google, start your own YouTube channel, try to master TikTok, or just include video as part of an email campaign, you should know that you are harnessing a medium your customers are already engaging with and deriving huge pleasure from. Here's just a few of the reasons that video works so well as a medium:

▶ Video catches people's attention far more than static content ever will. It enables your brand to stand out in a noisy landscape where your competitors might still be using static imagery and copy.

▶ You can give your customers a huge amount of information in a short, compelling way that maximises their time.

► Video engages the viewer's senses through sight and sound to deliver a more gratifying sensory experience.

► It helps build trust in your brand, validating your products and reinforcing your brand image.

► Through video, you can stir emotions, bringing people moments of pleasure or reducing them in an instant to compassion or sadness. This enables you to communicate with your customers on a far deeper level and to create an emotional connection that makes them 'feel' something about your brand.

► Video is the ultimate vehicle for storytelling. You can capture your audience's imagination, transporting them away for a moment and engaging them in your world.

► **Video creates greater impact, is more memorable and ultimately leads to better purchase decisions in your customers (with more comments and shares achieved for a lower cost per click).**

The great news is that many brands are still engaging in old-fashioned marketing techniques like TV, print and radio, despite the clear evidence that digital is more effective. Even so, of the one-third who are investing in video marketing, most have failed to unleash its full potential. This means the video space is still hugely up for grabs and, if you get your strategy right, you can make your brand thrive.

"

WHEN YOU TELL A
STORY THROUGH VIDEO
THAT RESONATES DEEPLY
WITH YOUR AUDIENCE, YOU
WILL NOT ONLY CAPTURE
THEIR ATTENTION BUT YOU
WILL POSITION YOUR
BRAND IN A COMPLETELY
DIFFERENT LIGHT.

"

For those brands that are forward thinking and embrace a video-first strategy, success follows quickly. Red Bull, Patagonia and Lego are all examples of brands that have thrived through transforming themselves into video content publishers. They all have incredible YouTube channels that are a must-have destination for fans. They not only have a loyal tribe of followers who buy in to their entire ethos as a brand, but they also dominate their sector with brand recognition that transcends the products they sell. The longevity that comes with this strategy has secured these brands a bulletproof status that seems impossible to shake.

In 2014 feminine hygiene brand Always created a video titled 'Like a Girl' that was designed to drive conversation around women's self-esteem. I won't spoil it for you by giving too much detail, but it put women on camera to talk about what that phrase means to them. The film is an emotional watch and the message is powerful. It went viral, with over 90 million views and 4.4 billion media impressions. Not only that, but it actually made a real difference to people's perceptions. A study found that 70% of women and 60% of men claimed that 'The video changed my perception of the phrase "like a girl"'.[12,13] I'm a recent father of a baby girl who I hope will grow up to be strong and confident. Rewatching that video as part of the research for this book literally brought a tear to my eye. That's the power of video.

The brands that are leading the way in video content creation achieve something very few manage to do: they create content that truly resonates with their audience. It's this resonance that has propelled them into the spotlight and made them stand head and shoulders above their competition. When you tell a story through video that resonates deeply with your audience, you will not only capture their attention but you will position your brand in a completely different light. You can form bonds with them that go far beyond traditional advertising. Think about the video you could be creating for your brand; how can it revolutionise your business?

CHAPTER 2

THE BATTLE FOR YOUR CUSTOMERS' ATTENTION

YES, IT'S A BATTLE

Globally, digital advertising budgets now exceed spend on all other media. Think about that. As a global industry of marketers, we have collectively come to the conclusion that you get better return on investment (ROI) from digital than from all other offline tactics, including print, out of home, radio and TV. We know that people are spending more time online than ever before and, because most of that time is spent on smart devices, we can reach them more effectively than any other means at our disposal. But this presents a problem.

Spoiler alert! You aren't the only brand trying to communicate with your customers. There's a battle raging for their attention. With so many brands competing in such a confined environment as the internet, the noise has risen to eardrum-splitting levels. I use the term 'confined' because, despite the vast expanse of the internet and the possibilities it presents, most of us hang out in the same places. This is largely due to the outrageous global monopolies that have been allowed to develop: 92% of all internet searches are made on Google[14] and only a handful of companies can make it onto page 1 of the search results. Only around 6% of people browse beyond the first page of results,[15] giving rise to a well-known SEO experts' joke that goes: 'Where's the best place to hide a body? The second page of Google.'

When we're not searching, we are either on Facebook or Instagram (owned by the same organisation, by the way), Twitter or LinkedIn. 80% of us watch videos on YouTube, a platform with 2.1 billion users.[16,17] We read the same free online newspapers and magazines. We all shop on Amazon or other popular online retailers, where we relish the prospect of ordering something that can be delivered to our door the next day. And the entire time we're doing all this, our every move is being tracked by cookies so we can be advertised to, based on our demographic and interests. We also get followed around the internet being retargeted by something we've already shopped for (never look for an engagement ring on a shared computer, by the way). It's estimated that on average we are exposed to 4,000 commercial messages every single day.[18,19] We are being bombarded day and night with advertising, and do you know what? It's starting to piss people off!

We are all starting to become experts at tuning out online adverts. In the same way that you can choose to go and make a cup of tea during the TV ad break, so too can you find ways to avoid seeing online adverts – whether that's by ignoring a display ad that appears next to a website by putting it in soft focus in your peripheral vision, or switching to another browser window while YouTube tries to play you a pre-roll advert. When Facebook tries to play an advert to you midway through a video you are enjoying, you just scroll down the feed to look at your friend's latest pictures while you wait for it to finish. We're so sick of advertising that one-third of us now routinely use ad blockers.[20] And subscription news and magazine sites are gaining in popularity because they don't have adverts; look no further than Netflix and Hulu for confirmation of this. This consumer trend is being listened to, and Apple has now banned third-party cookies in its Safari browser, preserving its users' privacy so they can't have their data shared around by advertisers. And in January 2020, Google announced that it would be following suit on its Chrome browser.[21]

But why am I saying all this when I'm a massive advocate for the power of video and digital marketing? Because I want to hammer home the point that, up until now, we've had it easy. The brave new world of digital marketing was a doddle. Anyone with decent SEO skills could get their website to the top of a Google search. A small business with a smidgen of Facebook advertising knowledge and a tiny budget could propel itself forward, and a half-decent video could go viral with millions of views. But that was then, and this is now.

Because the marketing world is migrating its advertising spend to online, it's beginning to create a vastly oversaturated space. Right now, there are still opportunities to advertise on Facebook and Instagram quite affordably, but that window is closing. As more big brands begin to plough their marketing budgets into this space, they're going to drive up the cost of advertising and create a highly competitive environment. Unless you have an endless budget, only the best creative content will shine through to compete in this space.

Ad fraud is also becoming a major problem for advertisers. This is where criminals use a variety of sophisticated tools to defraud businesses of their advertising budget. It's a complicated concept that I can't fully unpack here, but on a basic level: you think you are paying to show your advert to your customers, but the money is being siphoned off into the criminal's pocket. It's such a lucrative business that it has now become the second largest source of income for organised crime after narcotics, worth an estimated $36bn a year globally.[22] Both the widespread adoption of digital advertising by bigger businesses and the huge increase in advertising fraud have led to more expensive advertising that is decreasing in its efficiency.

"

STOP THINKING OF
YOURSELF AS AN
ADVERTISER AND
THINK OF YOURSELF
AS A PUBLISHER.

"

In my view, the old ways of whacking your customer over the head with an advert shouting about your brand don't work as well when you move them online. To grab your customers' attention, you need to create video content that they will actually enjoy, appreciate and engage with. Stop thinking of yourself as an advertiser and think of yourself as a publisher. When you do that, and start giving back to your customers, you will win their loyalty in return. That's how you build a tribe and future-proof your brand. To compete, the modern marketer has to work harder and be far craftier. To dominate this space, you will need to harness the power of video marketing.

STRATEGY WILL GET YOU IN THE TOP 1%

So what is 'video marketing'? What does that term actually mean? Simply put, video marketing is the idea that any piece of video content needs to be surrounded by a solid marketing strategy. The video needs to have a clear purpose to it. It should be tied to your business objectives, centred around your customers and supported by digital marketing. I say to our clients that 'video for video's sake doesn't work' – by that, I mean that you can create an outstanding piece of video content, but if you don't have a video marketing strategy around it, then it probably won't work.

If you are one of the few marketers who are getting consistently great results from video marketing, then congratulations, you are in the top 1%. If you aren't, then don't worry; we're going to get you there. The truth is that the vast majority of marketers don't know how to get the best results from video. Most assume that to have success with video marketing, all you need to do is create some video content that is beautiful and impactful. That you can just get the creative juices flowing, throw enough budget at it and let the content do the rest. They believe that a great idea is enough to make a video go viral, but that's just not the case.

For video to work well, you need to have a solid video marketing strategy around your project. It's essential; not having such a strategy is one of the biggest mistakes that marketers make when they are trying to harness the power of video. I know this because it's a mistake I made when I first started creating content for brands.

When I started my business Small Films, I had come from a 14-year career in the television industry. I was a creative through and through, producing and directing on prime time TV series, from cooking shows with celebrity chefs to documentaries about serial killers. I confess that I was perhaps quite naïve in the beginning, and possibly a bit arrogant. I thought that with my level of experience, I could just create appropriate promotional material and it would be enough for clients to start lining up to do business with us. But I quickly realised that creating high-quality video content wasn't enough. There were many more factors at play that contributed to the success of a campaign – from budget, time and resources to stakeholders, audience and distribution methods. It wasn't just about the way the campaign 'looked'. I came to see that even more important than delivering a lovely-looking video for our clients was the need to deliver them a result. And for video to deliver a result, it needs to be accompanied by a solid strategy.

Some of the very first clients we worked with received fantastic-looking videos with high production quality, but they either didn't know how to use them or they were communicating the wrong message to the wrong audience. One of the first videos we ever made was for a local clay pigeon shooting company. We threw the kitchen sink at it from a content creation perspective, capturing incredible shots of shotgun cartridges being ejected in slow motion and smoke streaming from gun barrels, as well as some epic aerial shots. We combined that with dramatic music, sound effects and premium motion graphics. The result was a high-impact, exhilarating two-minute video that encapsulated a typical day of clay pigeon shooting. I'm still proud of that video to this day, and the client was over the moon with the result. But when I look back, I realise there was a big part missing from this project; if I'd known then what I know now, I could have helped our client so much more.

The truth was that even though the client was very happy with the video, he didn't know how to use it properly. So he put it up on his website and social media and pinged it around to people who were interested in booking with his company. It got him some results and almost certainly delivered a good return on his investment. However, it could have done so much more for him. We could have chopped it up into 15-second adverts to run as Facebook and Instagram campaigns, as well as display adverts on local news websites or country and shooting magazines. We could have shot some additional material on the day, capturing some testimonials with happy customers that could have been included on his website to establish credibility and trust in the product. We could also have dug into some more details of the packages he offered, to help customers at the point of sale. Back then, we approached the project with the objective of creating a single piece of beautiful video that would look good and have impact. But we should have approached it with tangible objectives in mind, like sales and ROI.

We had a few more projects like that one back in the early days, where our role as the video company was only to fulfil the content creation part of the project. We had a brief and we'd just film and edit it to our best ability. But I would frequently see that, despite creating outstanding work, the videos would sit on the client's website doing not very much for them, or languish in the 'YouTube graveyard' (as I like to call it), where they would die a slow death because no one was visiting their channel. I began to realise that exceptional creativity without strategy leads to an ineffective video.

So it was at that point that I took off my creative hat and embedded myself in the business world of our customers. Once I truly understood their objectives, I was better able to see how video could fit into their wider marketing activity. By developing our own methodologies that married strategy and creativity, we were able to start producing exceptional results for our clients, which led to repeat business and the growth of Small Films. Within five years of starting the company, we'd won projects with some of the biggest brands in the country, including Aldi and EDF Energy. Today, when we engage with new clients, a big part of my job is to educate them about our unique offering as a business. I have to change their perception of us so that they understand we don't just send a video crew to film and edit based on a brief. We're a new breed of video agency that is results driven, putting video marketing strategy at the heart of all our work so we can deliver measurable outcomes for our clients. Great creative work isn't enough to get results. Having a solid strategy in place is absolutely fundamental if you want your video content to hit the mark.

Here are a few of the common mistakes I see brands making when they embark on a video project:

▶ Starting a video project with no real game plan, appearing haphazard or reactive. This leads to an unwieldy beast that is hard to control.

▶ Not tying the video project to business and marketing goals. Inevitably, this means it sits in a silo and doesn't support your wider objectives.

▶ Not understanding the desired outcomes or putting key performance indicators (KPIs) in place to track results. Without KPIs, you can't demonstrate success.

▶ Trying to appeal to too broad an audience without zeroing in on the customers you really want to reach. This leads to vanilla content that appeals to no one.

▶ Poorly executed content that doesn't stand out because the quality is bad. At best, it's just time and money wasted; at worst, it can reflect poorly on your brand.

▶ Uninspiring video with bad storytelling that doesn't engage the audience. You need to add a bit of drama to even the most mundane videos. Without it, people will switch off after a few seconds.

▶ Creating video and then just 'hoping for the best', even waiting for the video to go viral rather than putting time and effort into amplifying its impact with digital marketing. Surprise, surprise: the best video in the world won't work unless people see it.

When marketers attempt a video project and the results are lacklustre, they seem surprised and then blame the medium itself, claiming that video is just too expensive and time consuming, with poor ROI. The truth is that if you make even a few of the common mistakes I've just listed, the likelihood is that your video content won't do the job you wanted it to do. That is a huge shame because – when you get it right – video can deliver unbelievable results. I want to help you avoid making the same mistakes that 99% of marketers make when trying to master video, so that you make video marketing a regular and dependable part of your marketing mix.

Remember that it's a noisy world out there, and the war for your customer's attention is raging. The battlefield is littered with the carcasses of household-name brands who couldn't keep up with the changing times. Woolworths, Mothercare, Debenhams, HMV, Blockbuster, Topshop, Borders, Comet; the list goes on and, very sadly, keeps growing. And it's not just bricks-and-mortar stores that are under threat. Just because you have a great online presence doesn't mean you are future-proofed. The online playground has got much tougher, and there are a lot more bloodied knees. Even bigger marketing budgets don't necessarily guarantee your position in the spotlight. With consumers becoming more and more 'turned off' to online advertising, all of us marketers have to work a lot harder to win the trust and wallets of our customers. And that's where video comes in.

CHAPTER 3

HOW VIDEO CAPTURED MY IMAGINATION

'm really excited to take you on this journey into creating resonance with your video content and I hope that, after reading this book, you'll be as passionate about video storytelling as I am. I absolutely love the creative process of taking the germ of an idea and transforming it into a fully fledged piece of unique content that can communicate a single thought to millions of people. The power of the moving image is one of humankind's most incredible creations, and it's something I've been fascinated by from a very early age.

EARLY MAGIC

Because I was a child of the 80s, television played a big role in my childhood. I'd be glued to the TV set watching cartoons like *He-man*, *Transformers* and *Thundercats*. Films like *The Goonies*, *Crocodile Dundee* and *Indiana Jones* formed a seminal part of my childhood. I also loved watching Attenborough documentaries about lions on the Serengeti and great white sharks. Mum always said that if I was watching TV, no amount of shouting my name would get my attention. Unfortunately, my wife sometimes says the same thing...

My dad used to rent VHS camcorders (they were a thing back in the late 80s and early 90s) and bring them home to take family movies. Looking back at a few of these videos, I see that I spent most of my time jumping in front of the camera and pulling faces. But I always remember being fascinated by the home movie camera and asking Dad if I could play with it. It had a feature on it where you could make everything go pixelated in a kind of retro, high-tech way. I used to love that feature. When Dad finally purchased his own camcorder, he agreed to let me borrow it.

My creativity unleashed, I started to make my own movies with a friend. We recreated *The Terminator*, acting the parts ourselves and creating title cards using bits of cardboard and felt-tip pen. I even made a short stop-frame animation with little clay monsters. To make the animation, I had to press the 'record' button and immediately press 'stop' again so I got a split second of animation. I'd then move the characters a few millimetres and grab another split-second shot. Of course, these days I have an app on my iPhone that can create stop-frame animation in a jiffy, but back then it was a lot of work. Thinking back, I'd started my journey into the world of video content creation just through having access to that camcorder. Then I got my first lucky break.

We were encouraged by our school to do some work experience during the holidays, but I'd already done a stint at my dad's office (a meat processing company). That had been pretty dull, apart from the time he took me into the meat lockers with hanging pig carcasses; as a teenage boy, it was something I found morbidly fascinating. This second time, I was determined to find something more interesting to do. It turned out that Jake, a neighbour's son, was working as a cameraman for a TV company in London and he agreed to let me shadow him for a week. He was working for a Channel 5 entertainment news show with Sara Cox, so we ran around the capital doing news junkets with random celebrities, from Peter Andre to Nigel Mansell and even the boy band Blue. It was great fun and gave me a flavour of the world of television production. I'm very grateful to Jake for that experience, and he remains a friend to this day.

MY FIRST BREAK IN THE INDUSTRY

I decided to try to break into the industry so, after graduating from university with a degree in History and Spanish (and a diploma in Film Direction from Barcelona International Film School), I began ringing around every place I could think of that might give me a job in TV. After calling the History Channel and being rejected for what felt like the hundredth time, a friendly receptionist put me onto a job site for TV work. From there I got my first job, as an audience researcher for a company called Powerhouse. My role was to spend all day cold-calling a list of people who may or may not be interested in being an audience member on the live eviction days for the second-ever *Celebrity Big Brother*. So I spent my day getting a mix of 'Oh lovely, dear' and 'F*ck off!' from various members of the British public. Cold-calling was a horrible job, but as recompense I got to attend the live filming of the show, which was a great experience. I had to herd the audience members around the set, getting them to scream at the right moments and shut up at the wrong ones. That's the part I loved. And from there, I made my way in the world of television production.

Over 14 years, I worked my way up through the ranks of the television industry, from researcher and assistant producer to director and series producer. I travelled the world fishing with Robson Green, went to Cambodia on an adventure with Gordon Ramsay, and shot documentaries about the global heroin trade, serial killers and the Mafia. I filmed gypsy girls making wedding dresses in Liverpool and shamans performing traditional medicine in the deep Peruvian Amazon, and I watched Jamie Oliver collect a semen sample from a pig in front of a live audience on Channel 4. I worked both here in the UK and (for a few years) in the TV industry in New York, and I loved my job. I felt very lucky to have had the opportunity to see places and do things that

I will always remember and look back on. Throughout that time, I crafted my skills of storytelling using the moving image.

HEADING FOR THE 'TINY SCREEN'

I had seen the rise of digital video and watched its progress with fascination. I had seen the shift from TV to online viewing, with services like YouTube, iPlayer, Netflix and other video streaming services. I swiftly realised that the move to online video would present incredible opportunities for businesses looking to advertise. It would offer opportunities for a prolific amount of content that was previously not achievable with the budgets required for television advertising. As I saw the rise of online video, I also realised that the barrier to entry for video professionals was virtually non-existent. Anyone with a few hundred pounds could set themselves up as a videographer, and the quality of content being put out reflected that. It was at that point that I decided to set up my business and to bring the skills and expertise of television making on the 'small screen' to the 'tiny screen' of people's laptops and phones.

So in 2016 I founded my agency, Small Films, with a simple yet powerful purpose: to help brands stand out in the online space with reliable, effective video powered by exceptional storytelling. Since then, we've worked with dozens of brands – from small businesses and start-ups like Emily Crisps and Plenish through to big brands like Aldi and EDF Energy. We've helped them to communicate with their customers better, from crowdfunding videos to infor-

**OUR BRAND AFFINITIES
ARE THE COMMON GLUE
THAT LINK US ALL
TOGETHER, REGARDLESS
OF AGE, GENDER, RACE
OR BACKGROUND.**

mational films, product explainer videos to social media content and digital advertising.

For me, making content for brands, rather than for TV channels, has not only been a natural fit, but something I absolutely relish. Growing up in the 80s and 90s, I was strongly imprinted by popular culture, and that also goes for the brands I was raised on. BMX, Weetabix, Frisbee, Nike, Levi's; they are all as much a part of my identity as where I lived or what school I went to, so having the opportunity now to make content for these kinds of brands feels like a real privilege. Our brand affinities are the common glue that link us all together, regardless of age, gender, race or background. Strangers can easily begin a conversation about their favourite clothing brand or connect over their love of cereal. I've had numerous conversations with different friends in pubs, ranking our favourite crisps or chocolate bars. We even share our experiences of new brands with each other, excited to give an 'inside track' on a new or exciting product. I believe that the brands we love deserve to be talked about and that those brands can make a positive impact on the world with the video content they create.

CHAPTER 4

THE RESONANCE METHOD

VIDEO IS THE BEST WAY TO CREATE RESONANCE WITH YOUR AUDIENCE

From the moment I stopped making TV shows and started making videos for brands, I began forensically examining our work to see which elements contributed to a successful project. I also looked long and hard at famous branded video campaigns and best-in-class work from the industry. I wanted to know what criteria led to an award-winning video, so we could keep improving what we were doing. What ingredients are essential if you want the best chance of success? And is there a secret to making a video go viral?

I put on my detective hat and looked at what budgets they had, who the director was, which cameras were used, the style of filming, and a whole host of technical elements that I felt were relevant to the video's success. But I soon realised that the success of a video (including whether it went viral) wasn't solely down to the technical execution of the video. Some big-budget productions with all the bells and whistles have average results, and some low-budget ones can do really well. There was far more at play when it came to video success.

I kept ruminating on this subject, considering all the different aspects of a good video, bouncing ideas off other content creators, and getting very mixed views. Some thought the camera work was most important; others thought it was all about storytelling. Some felt that having a gimmick was essential, while others thought gimmicks should be avoided. I frankly got myself into quite a head spin trying to get to the bottom of this burning question. I had to take a step back. I had to stop letting myself get bogged down in the minutiae of video content creation and this camera versus that camera or this filming technique versus another.

I began to think, 'What is the fundamental reason for creating video content for a brand?' And I found the answer was 'To tell a story about the brand to its customers'. Brands are telling their story to customers all the time in lots of different ways through text, imagery or audio, or in person through human interaction. In this case, the medium for telling the story is video. Video is just the technology that's being used. It's as simple as that.

Then I thought, 'When you tell any kind of story, what makes it a story that someone will listen to?' And a pretty simple answer came to me. I concluded that, regardless of the story you are telling– whether you are regaling your friends with tales of your trip to Thailand, writing a novel, shooting a Hollywood film, scripting a TV show, standing on stage, doing a live radio show or creating branded video content– the story that people will listen to is the story that resonates with them. When the story resonates with them, they pay attention, they engage with it, they remember it and they can retell it to their friends.

Creating resonance with your audience really is at the heart of all the best stories. Once I'd found that truth, I spent a very long time examining the key components that are essential for creating video that resonates with an audience. After a great deal of thought, effort and trial and error, I created the Resonance Method, my unique system for ensuring that your video content resonates with your target audience.

WHERE STRATEGY MEETS CREATIVITY

If you are like most marketers, then marketing for your brand often feels like an uphill struggle. Along with your enormous list of responsibilities, you are always trying to innovate– testing new things, exploring different tac-

> ## VIDEO ISN'T JUST A 'NICE TO HAVE'; IT MUST DELIVER RESULTS.

tics and technologies and reaching new markets. Budgets are spread thin and, no matter what you do, nothing ever seems to work quite as well as you thought it would. Marketing is tough these days, and the competition has never been hotter. However, when you create true resonance with your customers through your video content, you can convert their hearts and minds to your brand. And that makes everything else so much easier.

When we work with clients, they ask me all kinds of questions around how to use video. They want to know what type of video gets the best results, how long the video should be, which cameras are best, whether animation is better than live filming, how much it costs, how long it takes. I could write a list of 100 different questions I get asked about video. But while all these specific questions have a place, most of the time they aren't focusing on what really matters. I've said it before, but I'll say it again: video isn't just a 'nice to have'; it must deliver results. So the first question any marketer should ask when embarking on a video project is: 'What do I want to get out of this?'

I always ask that question whenever I speak to a new client. And I get answers around some of the things you might expect, like wanting to get millions of views, grow their social channels, drive sales or create brand uplift. The client might want to win awards, to create campaigns they are proud of, to get praise from their boss or even a promotion because of the video work they've done.

However, this often only scratches the surface of what they really want to happen. Because, if they are really honest with themselves, they know deep down that they don't just want more effective marketing. They want their brand to be the one everyone is talking about. They want their brand to be at the centre of conversation and to be loved by their customers. Ultimately, they want it to dominate their sector. When you create resonance with your customers through video content, all that is possible.

So how do you create resonance with your customers through your video content and convert them into loyal fans of your brand? The Resonance Method marries strategy and creativity to provide a simple yet robust framework for any successful video project – one that depends upon five key principles. If you approach video marketing concentrating on these five areas, your videos will have the best chance of success. Those areas are Vision, Idea, Drama, Execution and Outreach. (Yes, they neatly make 'VIDEO'. Aren't I clever?)

I'm going to break these down in detail for you in the following chapters, but here's a quick overview:

▶ **Vision** is about getting clear on your objectives for your video campaign, the audience you are trying to reach and the way you are going to measure the outcome of the campaign. This is to avoid wasting time, energy and budget on video projects that don't deliver a tangible result.

▶ **Idea** is about hooking the audience in with a great concept that will resonate with them. Through having the right idea, you can ensure your video stands out from all the other content that's competing for your audience's attention.

▶ **Drama** is about telling your story in a compelling way that will engage your viewer, and having the right people tell that story with energy so it's enthralling. Through expert storytelling, you will leverage your audience's attention in the right way, so they don't drop off within a few seconds of watching your videos.

▶ **Execution** is about creating maximum impact for your video by producing it at the highest quality possible for the budget available. High-quality video ensures your brand is represented in the right way and gets the most traction, so your videos are liked, commented on and shared.

▶ **Outreach** is about making sure your content is distributed in the right places and to the right audience, so they connect with it. Ensuring good Outreach avoids your videos fizzling out because nobody sees them. Ultimately, it's what will drive the results for your brand.

Think about these five areas as a whole, rather than a step-by-step process. When you are deciding on your Vision for the project, you should also be thinking about your Outreach. When you look at your Idea, you should also think about the Execution and how you will create Drama. Looking back at our most successful projects, they all resonated deeply with the audience. That's the reason they did so well. Even looking at well-known video campaigns we had nothing to do with, the hallmarks of the Resonance Method were there.

THE RESONANCE METHOD

▶▶ **V**ISION

▶▶ **I**DEA

▶▶ **D**RAMA

▶▶ **E**XECUTION

▶▶ **O**UTREACH

CASE STUDY

PUTTING A PHONE CASE BRAND ON THE MAP
THROUGH CUSTOMER RESONANCE

Mous were launching a new product onto the market: an indestructible iPhone case. They came to us for a video that could be used in an initial crowdfunding campaign and then for further promotion of the product.

Now, we could have just started plucking creative ideas out of thin air and assigned the best production team and cameras to capture impressive footage, but would that have led to game-changing success for Mous? The answer is no. Instead, we took the time to plan the project properly and take a strategic approach before we began getting creative.

We were absolutely clear on the Vision for the video and were laser-sighted in our strategy. We knew the market was crowded with competitors trying to offer similar products and we knew the early adopters would be the kind of iPhone fans who queue for hours outside the Apple store waiting for the latest release. These are fans who geek out on tech and do their online research before buying a product. Because we had a clear Vision, we were able to come up with the right Idea for a video that would reel in customers. We wanted dramatic stunts to grab their customers' attention, so we decided to drop real iPhones from a 45-foot crane onto concrete and from the top of Waterloo Bridge. We stress-tested the phone in other fun, real-world locations to add jeopardy and Drama. However, because we knew our audience were tech savvy, we also knew they would be sceptical. So we included the science behind AeroShock, the protective technology inside the case's core, using animation to demonstrate how it protected the phone.

Looking back at the Drama we injected into the video, we started by telling a story that tugged at the heart strings of our core audience of iPhone fans. We knew that iPhone owners care deeply about the welfare of their phones. They get frustrated by the fact that they buy a very expensive, sexy-looking iPhone and then end up having to cover it up with a huge brick of a phone case. However, they are so paranoid about dropping their phone and breaking it that they wouldn't risk a slim designer phone case that offers little protection. We set out the problem and introduced the ways in which this product solved it.

Crowdfunders also love to 'buy in' to the story behind the brand, so we put the founders on camera to talk about how they had left their salaried jobs behind and sunk blood, sweat and tears into this make-or-break venture. The story had a simple narrative arc and engaged the viewer throughout the video.

The video had impact because the Execution was also on point. The filming and editing were both done to a high standard, with the right music to create moments of excitement and energy. We coached the founders into a great performance, so they were both passionate and genuine. We also included a mix of styles, including some home-shot footage from early in their journey, footage from the iPhones as they were dropped, live filming on the street, well-lit studio shots, and some animation to bring the technology to life.

Finally, as well as having clear Vision, Idea, Drama and Execution, the video was supported by solid Outreach. The team at Mous were very sophisticated with their marketing considering the size of their company (a total of five back then). They had a daily countdown to the product launch on the crowdfunding platform Indiegogo, releasing snippets from the video on Facebook to get fans excited. They also ran paid adverts using the video to build up a mailing list of potential customers who were promised 'early-bird prices' when the product launched. This meant that, when the campaign went live on Indiegogo, they immediately had a huge number of sales. This guaranteed income, gave them the confidence to sink more and more money into paid advertising, and accelerated orders of the product. The paid advertising gave the video the boost it needed and enabled it to gather its own momentum so that they ended up with huge numbers of organic views.

Everyone knows someone who always breaks their phone, so this video really resonated with the audience. People engaged with it, shared it and tagged their friends in it.

The results were:

► Over 25 million views within a few months

► $2.5 million in pre-orders of a product that was still at prototype stage

► Mous grew from a team of five to over 40 people

► Ranked as one of Forbes's fastest revenue growth start-ups

► The video won the CVA Crowdfunding Video Awards.

Mous continues to use video as an integral part of its marketing strategy. I also bet that if you have an iPhone in your pocket right now, you'll probably be researching their cases.

Watch the video here:
https://youtu.be/49tFe9rVglM

Or scan this QR code:

Look at your favourite TV shows.

Time and again, I look at the most successful pieces of branded video content and I see the Resonance Method in abundance. It even echoes what we see on television. I realise now that we were also employing these techniques in making TV shows for years, even though to my knowledge no one took the time to put the methodology down on paper. Whether it's drama or a documentary, there are key components that ensure these shows resonate with the audience.

Allow me to share an example with you. I was one of the directors on BBC2's *Inside the Factory*, a series that went behind the scenes to find out how our favourite foods are made. It was presented by Gregg Wallace and Cherry Healey. In one of the episodes, we took viewers on a magical adventure to the factory of Swizzles Sweets, the makers of iconic sweets like Love Hearts and Drumstick lollies. (On a personal note, this was one of the most magical experiences of my working career; very Willy Wonka-esque and generally great fun.)

The Vision for this series was clear. It was a factual television series designed to appeal to a prime time BBC2 audience: a mainstream crowd and a coveted audience for the British television networks. Their Idea was to take viewers to places they would never otherwise get to see: behind the scenes in the factories that made their favourite foods. As well as Swizzles, we showed you how Kellogg's corn flakes, Walker's crisps and Heinz baked beans were made. In the case of the sweets episode, we teased the show up front, telling the viewer that we would show them how this factory pumped out 100 million sweets every single day, including Love Hearts and Drumstick lollies.[23] As well as the great Idea, the show had oodles of Drama, with a story that unpacked the nation's love affair with sweets, and filmed segments about the history of sweets, the science behind our addiction to them, and other fascinating titbits that provided colour, excitement and energy. All of this was underpinned by a 24-hour countdown timer that showed us how much a factory produced in a day. This added a bit of jeopardy to what could have been quite a conventional documentary series. The Execution was on point with experienced, high-energy presenters, the best film crews and cameras, and the best filming locations. And finally, the BBC didn't just rely on the series being a hit; they made sure to include Outreach by promoting it heavily, both on the channel and through PR and advertisements.

Of course, *Inside the Factory* has a certain magic that you can't quite put your finger on which has led to it being a rip-roaring success compared with other similar TV series.

The production company behind it, Voltage Productions, has created a prolific number of TV series, so they had the pedigree and experience to find this winning formula. However, ultimately, it's a series that really resonates with us, and much of that is to do with just a few simple ingredients that you can see in abundance.

WHAT HAPPENS WHEN YOU FAIL TO CREATE RESONANCE?

It may seem like I segued a bit there into the world of television programme making, but I want to drive home this point. When you create video content for your brand, you are fulfilling the same role that television production companies fill. You are creating video to provide your audience with value.

You might be advertising to them to inform them of new products or offers, you might be educating them with videos explaining the benefits you bring, or you might be entertaining them with content that positions your brand in a favourable light. Regardless of the type of content you create, your audience is at the heart of everything you do, so it's important that your content resonates with them. No, strike that– it's *essential*. When content doesn't resonate with an audience, it doesn't just lead to poor results; it can also be highly detrimental to a brand's standing and get them talked about in the wrong way.

To give you an example, Pepsi ran an advertising campaign that has become pretty famous in the marketing world as textbook bad practice. On the back of the Black

Lives Matter movement, Pepsi decided to create an advert featuring Kendall Jenner. In the advert, Kendall is seen on a fashion shoot while a protest is taking place on the street outside. It's getting heated, with aggressive exchanges between protesters and the police. Kendall takes off her wig, hands it over to her assistant (who happens to be black), grabs a Pepsi and heads out onto the street. She crosses over from the line of protesters, walks towards a police officer, opens the can and hands it to him. He smiles, and it defuses the violence that seemed sure to erupt.

I can only assume that the messages were intended to be 'Make love not war' and 'Everyone loves Pepsi'. However, whatever message this campaign was trying to communicate got lost in translation, and people reacted really badly. The Twitterverse exploded with hatred for Pepsi, which was seen as belittling the Black Lives Matter movement by suggesting that a privileged white model could diffuse months of race protests just by handing over a Pepsi. The advert did untold damage to the brand's reputation and they were forced to recall it.

It seems obvious to me that Pepsi had failed in the very first step of creating resonance with its customers. The team had sunk all their energy into creating impact through the Execution, with very high production quality and expensive talent, but they'd failed to think about the Vision of the campaign and who the audience was. If they'd taken time to put themselves in their audience's shoes, they might have considered that the audience's reaction to this message would be negative. They'd failed to realise that a message with Black Lives Matter as a theme would resonate with people who engaged with the movement – and people who engaged with this movement wouldn't appreciate its significance being belittled. Brands jumping on a 'purpose-driven' bandwagon is always a risky endeavour, and on this occasion it worked out very badly.

Creating resonance with your customers through video is difficult to accomplish without a systematic approach. In addition, telling a genuine story that will position your brand in the right way is a challenge without proper planning. However, when you get it right, the results can be game changing.

In the following chapters I'm going to break down each stage of the Resonance Method for you and provide a simple guide to making sure your videos have the best chance of success. Whether you are new to video or have already been using the medium but want to get better results, follow this guide and you will avoid some of the common pitfalls that marketers encounter when embarking on a video project. With this approach, you won't waste resources on an ineffective video. Not only that, but you will create videos that cut through the noise and grab your customers' attention. I'll also provide you with some simple exercises and checklists that you can complete. They will give you a video marketing roadmap for your brand and enable you to create a simple briefing document for your first video project. After that, it will be up to you to get out there and start creating. And remember... practice makes perfect.

Before we really get into it, I have a gift for you. Head over to **www.resonancebook.co.uk/starterpack** so you can download a bunch of free goodies that will get you started with video, including:

▶   Briefing document template

▶   Video mood board example

▶   Video script template

▶   Checklist: how to hire a production company

▶   Guide to digital channels for video marketing.

Make sure to use the briefing document to fill out the exercises I'll be giving you as we go through the Resonance Method. If you fill this out diligently, you'll have a fool-proof document to brief everyone on your team and any external suppliers for your next video project.

VISION

WHY YOU NEED VISION FOR YOUR VIDEO PROJECT

To have a successful video marketing strategy, it's essential that you start with a clear Vision for your project. This is about narrowing your focus and deciding on the entire purpose of this video campaign. Begin by asking yourself: 'What is my objective? Who is my audience? And what is the outcome I want to achieve?' Those three questions will act as your North Star to guide you through all the other aspects of the Resonance Method and form the bedrock of your video project.

It's really important that you get this right, because if you don't have a clear Vision from the outset, it will have all kinds of knock-on effects that will derail your work. This will ultimately lead to:

▶ A chaotic video project without a singular Vision, which then overruns and goes over budget

▶ A message that doesn't resonate with anyone because the audience hasn't been defined

▶ Poor-quality ideas plucked out of thin air because you haven't built solid foundations for your video project

▶ Being unable to track the success of the campaign because you didn't define your outcomes at the beginning

▶ Being held accountable for the perceived failure of the video campaign and not being trusted to do more video in the future.

CASE STUDY

LAUNCHING A PRODUCT WITH
VIDEO MARKETING

When we worked with Upbeat Drinks on the summer launch of their juicy protein water, they were really clear about the Vision for their project and had a solid understanding of their objective, audience and outcome:

▶ Their objective was to drive brand uplift and also generate sales.

▶ Their audience was young, female gym-goers and other health-conscious young professionals in London.

▶ The outcomes they wanted to measure were views, impressions and product sales.

Based on the overall Vision for the project, we came up with an Idea centred around a series of aspirational adverts that could work both online and offline. Drama was created by telling an aspirational story about a super-successful young woman who loved the product. The Execution was completed to the highest standard for the budget available, using a great camera crew, professional actors and intriguing locations. And finally, to achieve Outreach we brought a digital marketing agency into the project. Advertising centred around key Sainsbury's locations across the capital, with geotargeted Facebook, Instagram and YouTube advertising and digital billboards outside those stores, and we supported the campaign with photography that could be turned into print adverts on the London Underground. By focusing on specific Sainsbury's locations, rather than the entire capital, Upbeat was able to measure the sales uplift in those stores.

The results of the six-week campaign were:

▶ Over 2 million video views

▶ 4.5 million customer impressions

▶ 140% uplift in online sales

▶ A 30% increase in sales in store.

None of this would have been possible without a proper Vision for the project.

Watch the video here:
https://youtu.be/UCcWwmfLLjQ

Or scan this QR code:

HOW TO CREATE A VISION FOR YOUR PROJECT

Step 1: Set your objective

Video works best when there is a clear objective. When the objective is clear, the video can be produced in a tactical way to deliver the best results. That objective might be to make more sales or enable better purchase decisions, or it could be to launch a new product or reach a new market. I'm going to take a wild guess here and assume that you are embarking on this video project for a specific reason and to achieve an end goal, so think carefully about what the core objective is; try not to dilute the mission of the project by having too many objectives.

For example, we make product videos for Aldi's Special Buy department, with the objective of helping customers to make better purchase decisions when they are already shopping on the Aldi website. These products range from soup makers to slow cookers, log splitters to children's play tents. Because these videos have one job to do, they can do that job really well. They are about a minute long, concise, simple and informational. If they had to also work as adverts, we'd need to make them shorter and more attention grabbing. This would dilute their power as product videos. These videos resonate with the audience because they've been designed specifically for that audience. By having one objective to focus on, we help Aldi to frequently sell out of these products within a few days of them being listed.

Another example of having a clear objective for a video is when we make crowdfunding videos. The objective is to create a video that can help brands raise investment through crowdfunding platforms like Seedrs or Indiegogo. If you aren't familiar with these platforms, they are a great way to crowdsource funding from a large number of investors. We know that crowdfunding videos need more information in them to satisfy the concerns of potential investors, so they need to be longer and constructed differently to a product video. They are typically two to five minutes long and may contain detail about the company's financial health, product features or other information that will help convince the viewer to invest.

For example, we created a crowdfunding video for a technology platform aimed at property professionals. By including interviews with the team, key information communicated in motion graphics and other elements, we were able to help them raise nearly £1m in crowdfunding. This video worked really well for crowdfunding but couldn't double up as a video for their website; it would have been too long and detailed. Instead, we created a separate video for their homepage that was more stylised, aspirational and concise.

With crowdfunding videos, the objective is to raise money through investment. That's very different to when we create adverts for brands to make direct sales or raise awareness. In that instance, it would make more sense to create 15-second adverts and run a Facebook or Instagram digital advertising campaign. For example, we filmed a series of three adverts for Charlie Bigham's, the luxury ready meal company. The adverts featured the company's founder, Charlie, chatting with his head chef, Rupert, about the best side dishes to pair with their fish pie, beef pie and lasagne. These work really well as Facebook Ads for raising awareness of the brand, but wouldn't work as well on the company website as they don't go into enough detail.

Hopefully you can see that having a clear objective helps to inform the entire thrust of the video campaign. It will also enable you to home in on your audience and define the outcomes you hope to achieve with the project.

Common objectives for video campaigns

I've listed some of the most common objectives for video campaigns below. Try to have one primary objective that you are focusing on, and then one or two secondary objectives that align with it.

INCREASE SALES

If you sell your product direct to consumer via an e-commerce site or even a third-party retailer, then video can help you to increase your sales. Consider creating adverts for a digital advertising campaign or for digital billboards out on the street. For example, we worked with a bakery school to promote their online bakery classes ahead of Black Friday. The videos were simple. We showed the baked items you would learn to create, using some high-quality images and motion graphics, but through a targeted ad campaign on Facebook and Instagram we were able to generate a 4.5× return on advertising spend across the Black Friday period.

INCREASE LEADS

For marketers at business-to-consumer and business-to-business brands, increasing lead volume is often a major directive. That might mean filling the top of your funnel with leads for your sales team or increasing your email mailing list for regular offers and brand building. Using video as part of your content marketing strategy can be a great tactic if leads are your focus. Create videos that you know your customers will find useful, like webinars and e-learning courses. For example, we created an entire 37-chapter e-learning course about native advertising, delivered by experts from the advertising platform Taboola. Users can purchase the course via the freelancer recruitment site Fiverr, on their 'Learn with Fiverr' microsite. Taboola is a $2.6bn company, so they probably don't need the revenue from this $32 course, but the people downloading a course about native advertising are likely to be people who might use Taboola's platform in the future. That makes it a great lead-generation tool.

EXPLAIN PRODUCTS

If you have a complex product, or one with many features and benefits, a video can help your customers to better understand its value. Most customers would rather watch a quick video explaining your product than try to find the right information via your website.

RAISE BRAND AWARENESS

There are many brand-building exercises you can do with videos about the brand's story, through to filmed PR stunts or branded content. My key tip for increasing brand awareness is to create entertaining, educational or informative video that your customers will love to watch. However, sometimes it's just about getting people excited about your brand and the products you sell. We worked with Sock Shop to create a fast-paced, glossy brand film that celebrated their massive range of socks. It had the tag line 'Feel good from the feet up'. This video was used on the homepage and social channels and in general customer communication to get people excited about the brand.

EDUCATE CUSTOMERS

If you have a product that solves a problem, create a video that educates your customers about it. Often the customer doesn't even realise they have a problem to solve. For example, constant back pain can be caused by bad posture when sitting at a desk, but not many people with back pain realise that's the cause. So, if you have a product that's a standing desk, first educate your customers about the problem of desk posture before then telling them about your product.

CHANGE PERCEPTIONS

If you have an image problem, or just want to reposition your brand, video can be an incredible tool for achieving that. We frequently work with private schools in the UK who want to change the commonly held perception of their school. So, if they are seen as a 'sporty' school but want people to know they are also academic, then films about their curriculum can help change that. If they are historically known as a boys' school but are actually co-educational, then we'll create films about the opportunities for girls at the school.

BUILD AUTHORITY

Video is amazing for building authority in a particular sector. If you want to position your company as the 'go-to' experts for anything from financial advice to swimming pool installation, then release authoritative video content about this subject matter. You can also consider using your team members to talk on camera to help to build your personal brand. For example, we worked with EDF Energy, featuring their energy analysts talking on camera about all the latest changes to energy prices and forecasts for the future. We combined these interviews with statistics and animations on the screen. The videos positioned them as experts and provided useful insights for their customers.

INCREASE SEO

If you create videos answering questions that are commonly typed into Google, YouTube or other search engines, you can help your website get ranked for that search term. It's a great way of increasing traffic to your site. For example, if you are a brand in the DIY space, you could create tips and tricks for home improvements. If you sell beauty products, create tips and tricks on how people can look their best.

OPTIMISE CONVERSION RATES

If you are running an advertising campaign on Facebook, Instagram or Google, consider replacing your static ads with video ads. When you ditch photos and graphic design in favour of videos, you will see a lower cost per click and a higher return on ad spend (ROAS). In addition, if you are directing customers to a specific sales page, include a video on that page so they can get instant information.

GROW YOUR SOCIAL CHANNELS

Videos get better engagement and more likes, comments and shares than static posts, which is why a consistent video strategy on social media can bring huge rewards. Really think long and hard about the types of videos your customers will enjoy watching and how those videos will reflect your brand.

BUILD TRUST

In today's world of fake news, fake reviews and general fakery, customer trust is at an all-time low. The right video content can do wonders for helping customers to know, like and trust you. Videos featuring testimonials from customers, videos of your team, or case studies about your business can all be great trust-building exercises.

FIND NEW CUSTOMERS

Whether you are looking to penetrate a new market, territory, demographic or even just to poach customers from your competitors, video can be a great way to do it. A single video can be easily translated into multiple languages or re-versioned for different audiences. It's an efficient way of creating a useful marketing asset that can get immediate results. Couple this with geotargeted digital marketing campaigns and you can reach new markets quickly and easily.

HELP CUSTOMERS WITH PURCHASE DECISIONS

A simple one-minute product video used at the customer's point of purchase can often tip the balance in your favour. We are getting increasingly wary of making purchases online and being disappointed when the product doesn't live up to our expectations. These types of videos could feature on the product pages of your website, on third-party retailer sites (like Amazon), or even in physical displays in stores.

Step 2: Identify your audience

Once you've decided on your core objective and any secondary objectives that complement it, you can start to identify your audience. I can't overstate the importance of this stage. Understanding your audience is critical if you want to create content that will resonate with them. It's a common mistake to believe that if you try to appeal to as broad an audience as possible, you will get the maximum reach and the best results. This simply isn't the case. If you are trying to reach too broad an audience, you are in danger of your content being very vanilla and not resonating with anyone.

In the online space, the narrower and more niche you can get with your audience, the better. Even the biggest brands in the world, like Nike, Virgin or McDonald's, have their target market and know what will resonate with them. They may take a mass marketing approach, with high-level TV adverts and out-of-home campaigns, but the messaging and visual approach is designed to inspire their ideal customers. Coca Cola spends an average of $4bn per year on advertising,[24] but it still doesn't market to everyone. Its Christmas TV advert 'Holidays Are Coming' works well

"

IN THE ONLINE SPACE,
THE NARROWER AND
MORE NICHE YOU
CAN GET WITH YOUR
AUDIENCE, THE BETTER.

"

before *The X Factor* because the brand is associated with excitement, aspiration and fun; it wouldn't work so well before the *Antiques Roadshow*.

The video content that will have the greatest impact online is highly relevant to the audience you are trying to reach. So, if you are a men's watch brand releasing a new product that is only affordable to affluent individuals, then target them with relevant video content about luxury lifestyles. If you're a company making vitamin supplements for pregnant women, target your audience with content around the stages of pregnancy. It doesn't matter whether you have a chain of garden centres, a new fintech product, a children's charity or a food brand – the content you create must speak directly to your ideal customer. If you do that, you'll have the best chance of success.

Here's a hypothetical example. Imagine you are a brand that sells a high-tech food processor. You decide that a great video will be just the ticket to achieving more sales. You hire a great production company to shoot the video and assign a decent budget, but you don't do any work to identify your audience. The production company does a great job, and the finished film looks great. You are really happy with it, so you put it up on your website and social media channels, then sit back and wait for the sales to fly in. But nothing happens. It doesn't make any sense; the video makes the product look so good, so what went wrong?

It turns out that because you didn't identify the audience you were selling to, the production team chose to shoot the product on a neutral background that would appeal to as broad an audience as possible. The result is that no one finds it particularly relevant. You took advice from the technical department and loaded the video with reams and reams of technical specs and detail, which has led to an over-complicated product video that fails to identify the real benefits to the customer, such as saving time because it's the fastest, most sophisticated blender on the market and the easiest to wash up. Instead, the content is vague and doesn't sell the product properly.

Now imagine you take a different approach. You take the time to really understand your audience. You discover that your ideal customers are actually professional chefs in commercial kitchens. For them, the benefits of this product are obvious. Their pain points align perfectly with the product features, because they are time poor and want a product that's professional, versatile and top of the range. Now you can craft a story that talks to them about how they, as professional chefs, could make their lives a whole lot easier by having this blender. You might even decide to shoot the video in a professional kitchen, so it feels more relevant to them.

When you release the video, you also now know who it's aimed at, so you have a better plan for Outreach. Rather than just posting it on social media, you actively send it out via email to a list of 20,000 commercial kitchens across the country. Surprise, surprise – the sales start rolling in.

Step 3: Define the outcome

You know your objective and the audience you are targeting – but now you need to define the outcome you want from this video campaign. It's time to draw up some metrics so you can benchmark the success of your campaign.

This is the exciting part. This is the bit where you lay out exactly what could be achieved if this video project is successful. You can start to visualise exactly where it's going and imagine yourself standing in front of your team, boss, board or other stakeholders, pointing at juicy statistics on a slide deck. Or, if the idea of presenting to anyone scares the hell out of you, maybe you're sending an email on a Friday with your report, congratulating everyone on the success of the video campaign.

It's a common misconception that the impact of video cannot be measured. Video can absolutely be measured, and measuring impact is critical. You need to be able to prove to yourself and other stakeholders in the business that this has been successful and is worth doing again. Understanding the desired outcome for your video will also help you to define your investment in the project. And when I talk about investment, I don't just mean budget; I'm also talking about the time and energy you want to put in.

Without fail, when I'm speaking to a potential new customer about a video project, they ask me, 'How much does a video cost?' It's a perfectly reasonable question, but it's also an impossible one to answer. I usually respond with, 'That depends' – which isn't meant to be cryptic, vague or misleading. The truth is that video can cost anything from a few hundred pounds to hundreds of thousands, depending on your ambition for the project and desired outcome.

There are so many factors influencing the budget that you need to know what the goals are for the project before allocating the right resources. So ask yourself, 'What do I want to get out of this?' and 'What sort of video budget would feel appropriate to achieve that?' If your objective is to generate £1m in sales, then it might feel appropriate to spend tens of thousands on some video adverts. However, if this is just some quick behind-the-scenes shots of your latest store opening, you might decide to shoot it yourself on an iPhone. Think about your objective and the outcome you hope to deliver, then try to assign value to that outcome. When you understand the value of the outcome, it's a lot easier to decide on the budget, time and resources you will need to achieve it. Does that make sense?

If you want to know more about how much a video costs, visit:

WWW.SMALLFILMS.COM/HOW-MUCH-DOES-VIDEO-PRODUCTION-COST/

So, let's get into all the different ways that you can measure the success of your video project. But before we do, a word of warning. Don't fall into the trap of only focusing on 'vanity metrics' like views or customer impressions. These have their place in many instances, but they aren't the be-all and end-all of a successful video campaign. Some videos might only get a few hundred views, but if those few hundred views are by the right people, it could create a huge impact for your business. We get overly fixated on getting millions and millions of views in the online space, but just imagine if you were standing up at a conference and presenting to 1,000 people. Imagine the effect that could have for your business. And yet many marketers are disappointed when they get fewer than 1,000 video views.

For example, we created four videos for a business consultant who was selling to leaders in the pharmaceutical industry. Each new client was worth thousands of pounds to her business, and her target list for direct outreach contained fewer than 100 prospects. In this instance, her plan for Outreach to her customers was via video brochures in the post. These are brochures made from card which have small TV screens inside them. Terrible for the environment, but highly effective at grabbing someone's attention. That super-targeted approach led to greater impact than if she'd tried to get thousands of views online.

Tie your outcomes to the objectives for the video campaign and create some KPIs to evaluate your success. Let's look at some common outcomes to measure.

Common outcomes

Here are some of the most common outcomes you can deliver through a video project. Try to think creatively about what outcomes would be considered a success for your business. Then try to assign KPIs to those outcomes.

DIRECT SALES

The ultimate metric. If you are running an advertising campaign to drive sales, track those sales. Consider doing a test by running two adverts in parallel: one with video and one with a static photo. Measure how the video performs. At the risk of teaching you to suck eggs, don't forget to work out your profit margins for the advertising budget. It's one of the best feelings when you can show that you made a 5× or 10× ROI through a video campaign.

LEADS

If the video is driving customers over to a lead-capture form or signing up to your newsletter, then this is a simple metric to measure. Consider how much each lead is 'worth' to the business. Set the number of leads you want to capture as a result of your video campaign.

SALES CLOSE RATE

If you have a sales team that is taking marketing leads and trying to close them, your sales close rate is a great metric to measure. By arming the team with sales assets like customer testimonial videos, case study videos and explainer videos, you will find that it both shortens their sales cycle and leads to better conversion rates.

SOCIAL MEDIA GROWTH

Track the number of followers on your social channels after you start your video campaign. Set yourself a target and try to hit it. Measure the engagement levels on your videos to evaluate the impact they are having on your social media growth. Then consider 'boosting' your videos with some paid advertising for your social channels.

CUSTOMER ENGAGEMENT

As I said, video views are not the be-all and end-all. Look at customer engagement with your videos. Are people commenting, liking and sharing? Measure those metrics and also pull out some of the best comments about your videos; these are great to include as anecdotal examples of the video's success. You can also measure what proportion of your video people are watching before dropping off. How many are making it to 50%, 75% or to the end? YouTube is a particularly good tool for this.

RETURN ON AD SPEND

If you are running an advertising campaign and your objective is to lower your customer conversion costs, then measure the impact of adding video to your campaign. Typically, videos lead to lower costs per click, so you get a better return on your advertising spend. You can include stats on your average cost per click, cost per thousand impressions and cost per conversion.

VIDEO VIEWS AND IMPRESSIONS

Measuring your view count and impressions is a simple way of showing the effectiveness of your videos. If your objective is generating brand awareness and increasing the maximum number of people who are exposed to your brand, this is a great metric to measure. Don't just measure the views and impressions you've paid for– also measure your 'earned views'. These are the organic views that have come from people sharing your content.

AD RECALL

Measuring ad recall is a good way to assess the impact of your advertising. Generally speaking, this looks at how many people would remember seeing your advert if you asked them two days later. Both Google and Facebook offer this as a feature on their platforms, where they survey customers two days after watching an ad. The better the advert and the more it resonates with your audience, the more likely they are to remember it.

PRESS MENTIONS

It's a huge win to have your content featured by journalists. What would be the equivalent cost to advertise on their platform? And how many 'free views' have you achieved of your video by being featured in the news? We often work with PR agencies where the entire purpose of the video is to create a newsworthy piece of content for their clients.

AWARDS

Prestige is important when it comes to business. It establishes you as a key player and gives you free publicity. Winning awards using well-executed video content is a great way to draw attention to your brand and also to increase team morale. It's often the icing on the cake for a successful campaign – and there's nothing like getting dressed up in your glad rags and celebrating at the awards ceremony.

SEARCH ENGINE RANKINGS

If you create a video that's designed to answer your customers' problems, you have a good chance of improving your search engine rankings. Assess where your site or particular page ranks before and after the video is completed.

WEBSITE TRAFFIC

If you are creating content that points back to your website, make sure to measure your website visitors. A well-executed video can help your search engine rankings and increase the volume of traffic to your site.

FEEDBACK

This is not to be underestimated. If the CEO loves your content, or you are mentioned by key influencers in your market, that's a win. If customers comment on the video or hint at how useful they found it, make a note. Collect this feedback to include in your report after the campaign winds up.

QUALITATIVE AND QUANTITATIVE RESEARCH

If your objective is to change the perception of your brand or raise brand awareness, consider commissioning some research before and after your campaign to see if you have made any impact on your customers.

PERSONAL GOALS

I know we're talking about brand success here but, let's be honest, sometimes you want to give yourself a leg-up too. When the brand does well, you do well, so think about what you got out of this. Was the process enjoyable and stress free? Did you avoid long work days and sleepless nights? Did you get praise from your boss or team? Did any personal fame come from it, like speaking opportunities, media interviews or an invitation to the company ski trip? Could a bonus, pay rise or promotion be on the cards? Just make sure you don't put your personal goals on the video project briefing document!

By defining your desired outcomes and the way you will measure them, you can gather all the information into a 'post-match analysis' after the project is complete. You can bring that to all the other stakeholders and show your success. If you can, try to bring it all together by also focusing on whether the project was completed on time, within budget and with a proven ROI. If you can say that 'For every £1 we spent on video, we got £10 back', very few people are going to be able to argue with you.

Really take the time to get clear on your Vision for your video project with your objectives, audience and outcomes. It will form the bedrock of your campaign and enable you to come up with a killer Idea for your video.

TOP TIPS

1. Use video tactically to achieve specific goals.

2. Get clear on your Vision for the project and stick to it so you stay on track.

3. Settle on just one or two core objectives rather than diluting your impact by trying to achieve too many goals.

4. Be laser-sighted with your audience to avoid vanilla content.

5. Video isn't just a 'nice to have'. Get clear on the desired outcome of the campaign and set KPIs.

6. Don't just focus on vanity metrics such as views, likes and comments. Look for more tangible results like leads, sales and customer acquisition.

Create a briefing document so you can get the team and stakeholders aligned on your Vision.

START YOUR BRIEFING DOCUMENT

Have a think about your Vision for this project and then fill out the first part of your briefing document. If you haven't got yours yet, head over to **www.resonancebook.co.uk/ starterpack** now as we'll be filling it in as we go along. You can watch a video I recorded about the importance of a good briefing document here: **www.resonancebook.co.uk/videos**

VIDEO PROJECT
BRIEFING DOCUMENT

PROJECT OVERVIEW

The objective of this video project is to (*add objectives*):

....

....

....

AUDIENCE

Our audience is (*provide a clear description*):

....

....

....

OUTCOME

These are our objectives for the project, with KPIs (*list your KPIs for measuring the success of the campaign*):

....

....

....

Visit **www.resonancebook.co.uk/starterpack**
for a digital version of this briefing document.

IDEA

WHAT'S THE BIG IDEA THAT WILL MAKE YOUR CUSTOMERS TAKE NOTICE?

All videos need to start with a good Idea that will resonate with your customers. It's the big promise you are making to your customers and the reason why they would bother to watch your video. In the busy lives we lead, where the time we spend online is snatched and fleeting, we don't have energy to investigate things further unless we feel it's going to be worth our while. It's not up to your customers to watch your video on the off-chance that it might be useful; it's up to you to give them a damn good reason to watch. Actually, scratch that. It's up to you to make them believe this is a piece of content they cannot live without.

"

**IT'S NOT UP TO YOUR
CUSTOMERS TO WATCH
YOUR VIDEO ON THE
OFF-CHANCE THAT IT
MIGHT BE USEFUL.**

"

If you try to create video content starting from a bad initial idea, it will be hard to recover from it, because:

▶ A bad Idea can leave a stale taste in your customers' mouths because it has drawn their attention for all the wrong reasons

▶ Your audience will feel indifferent about your message and will ignore you

▶ Your team and suppliers will find it hard to get behind the project, because they won't believe in it

▶ The whole project will constantly feel like you are trying to fit a square peg into a round hole

▶ It's common to feel a personal sense of responsibility for a bad Idea that leads to a wasted opportunity, even if it was a team effort.

Coming up with a good Idea for your video isn't always about creating something mind-blowing or highly innovative; far from it. Often, it's just about focusing the mind on creating a simple Idea that's executed well and will resonate with your audience. It could be as simple as a 'Message from our founder' or 'Meet our team' – but delivered in the right way, in the right place, to the right audience, that Idea could have a huge impact. When you come up with a good Idea for your video, it will stand out from all the other uninspiring content that your customers are being exposed to. It will pique their curiosity, shock them, or make them laugh, cry or think more deeply. They'll engage with your video, talk about it and share it with their peers. It will lead to more attention, better views and ultimately much better results. The videos with the best Idea are often the ones that go viral.

When you start with a good idea, everything else will follow. I once made a documentary series called *Drugs, Inc* about the global narcotics trade. The Idea for this series was that we got access to film with drug-dealing kingpins and their crew. For the episode about the global heroin trade, I talked my way into a crack house in Chicago's West Side, where I filmed a local gang member chopping up a huge pile of heroin and dividing it into baggies he could sell on the street. I asked him if he had any remorse about being a heroin dealer and he said, 'No – I'd sell to your mother.' We took that soundbite and included it in the opening few seconds of the episode. It hooked the viewers and made them want to find out more. The Idea for this series was so good that everyone involved could see it would be success-ful before we'd even picked up a camera. I filmed the first series of *Drugs, Inc* but it went on to seven more series,[25,26] eventually being bought by Netflix and renamed *Dope*.

Coming up with ideas for a piece of video content that will resonate with your audience can seem like an intimidating task, but not when you follow the simple pro-cess I'm going to share with you and brainstorm ideas from a strategic foundation. We're going to define the type of content you are creating, get to grips with your audience, and then brainstorm ideas.

HOW TO COME UP WITH AN IDEA FOR YOUR VIDEO PROJECT

Step 1: Define the type of video content you are creating

Remember, you've already defined your Vision for this project. You know your objective, audience and outcomes, so you aren't just plucking ideas out of thin air. You are basing it on your strategic goals.

Which of the two content categories do you want?

There are lots of different types of video content you could create, from adverts to explainer videos and from animations to social media content, but I like to break video content into two categories:

1. Adverts

2. Branded content

Adverts are the type of video content that needs a paid advertising budget if you want it to work. In the same way that it would be pointless to create an advert for TV unless you also paid for the TV advertising spot, you also need an advertising budget for adverts in the online space. Whether it's an advert for Facebook or YouTube, or display advertising on Google, if you don't pay to show it to customers, it won't work.

Branded content, on the other hand, is video content that doesn't need an advertising budget in order to work. This is video content that is usually either entertaining, educational or informative. It is likely to build its own organic momentum by viewers engaging with and sharing it. An example would be informational videos that build up a picture of your brand and products. These videos are useful for customers who are looking for more information.

Now, it's not quite as black and white as this. Some adverts can go viral and gather their own organic momentum, and branded content will often benefit from having a paid advertising budget behind it. But in general, most content fits into one of these two main categories. So, first of all you need to decide whether you are advertising with your video or whether it is content for your brand. Once you've answered that question, we can go a bit deeper into the different types of video within the two categories.

The different types of adverts

If you are creating adverts for your brand, it's more than likely that you're trying to direct your customers to an action – buying your product, downloading a brochure, requesting a quote or generally signalling interest in your product or service. Depending on your business, you may be looking to reach your customers in all kinds of different online locations, from social media to popular websites, and from smartphone apps to VOD (video on demand) television channels.

Regardless of how you are planning to reach your customers, it's important to think about where they are in their buyer journey. By that, I mean: are they deep in 'shopping mode', having done their research and now feeling ready to buy? Are they still considering the different products and weighing up which one is best? Or have they never even heard of your product and don't even know they need it yet? Knowing your customer's state of mind and their level of purchase intent is crucial because that's what will inform your ideas for your video.

Generally speaking, for simplicity, I divide adverts into four categories:

▶ **Brand awareness:** making customers aware of you

▶ **Education:** making customers understand the problem you solve

▶ **Sales:** acquiring new customers with a direct call to action

▶ **Nurture:** selling to existing customers

It's important to tie the Idea for your advert to the objective of your video so you know what 'job' it has to do. For example, if your company sells Christmas hampers through an online store, you might want to create adverts for general brand awareness in September and October, just to make shoppers aware of your brand. Then in November and December you run adverts that educate your customers about how your product can save them the hassle of visiting the shops. You could then progress to serving them an advert that says 'Buy Now', alongside a discount code. And you could follow up with existing customers, providing offers on other products you sell throughout the year.

Knowing what type of advert you are creating is important because it will inform the placement of those adverts when it comes to working with your media buying agency or handling the digital marketing yourself. An objective of brand awareness will lead to a different style of advert and different placement of the advert than if you are looking for a direct call to action, like 'Buy Now'.

The different types of branded content

'Branded content' is quite a broad term that can refer to practically any type of content created by brands as part of their content marketing strategy, including blogs, podcasts and social media posts. But for the purposes of this book, when I refer to branded content, I'm talking about video.

In essence, branded content is video that offers some form of value to your customer, usually by being entertaining, educational or informative. Branded content could be a PR stunt you've filmed to create some buzz around your brand, or it could be a video for your homepage that talks about your brand manifesto. It might be YouTube content around a subject that your customers enjoy, or it could be some social media videos with tips and tricks. Branded content can benefit from being promoted using your advertising budget, but it doesn't always need to be. Branded content should stand on its own as an engaging piece of video, without the need for a big advertising budget.

I'm going to turn to YouTube for a simple explanation of the three broad categories of branded video content. While their description is focused on growing your YouTube channel, the principles can play out across all your other platforms, from your website to social media. They refer to this strategy as 'Hero–Hub–Help', and it should help you to come up with ideas for your video campaign. By the way, I've recorded a video about this topic that you can watch here: **www.resonancebook.co.uk/videos**

The three types of content are:

▶ **Hero:** attention-grabbing content for brand awareness

▶ **Hub:** regular content to engage your audience

▶ **Help:** video content that provides answers to common questions

'Hero' content includes videos that cause a big splash and get customers to notice you. In YouTube's case, it's about driving people to your channel. But maybe your objective is to drive traffic to your website, social media channels or other location where you can then leverage your customers' attention. Hero content tends to consist of PR-worthy, high-impact, attention-grabbing videos. They need to make as big a noise as possible, so you get your customers' attention.

'Hub' content is regular video content that gives them a reason to stay engaged with you. On YouTube this tends to be episodic, recurring videos that people come back to time and time again. You could also replicate this principle across your social media channels or if you were delivering regular content via an email newsletter. It keeps customers in your 'nurture pool' and keeps them engaged with your brand.

Finally, 'Help' refers to videos that answer customer questions. In YouTube's case, people are searching for answers to common problems via the search bar. Providing those answers in your videos helps drive people to your YouTube channel. The entire time, you are providing value to the viewer so they are encouraged to subscribe. Extending the 'Help' category further, this would include any informational films about your brand and products that you think your customers might be searching for. These could be on your website or another of your customer access points.

I'll give you a really quick example of how this plays out within YouTube. Red Bull are known as the kings of content marketing. The product is an energy drink, but we know the brand as so much more than that. It goes hand in hand with extreme sports, from wingsuit skydiving to soapbox go-kart racing – even a Formula 1 team. Red Bull's YouTube channel is a must-have destination for extreme sports fans, and video content is the cornerstone of their marketing.

When base jumper Felix Baumgartner wanted to attempt the world's highest skydive, Red Bull jumped at the chance to be involved.[27] Felix went up in a space capsule 24 miles into the atmosphere. Then, fully kitted out in a space suit, he jumped out, free-falling for over four minutes. And Red Bull filmed the entire experience. The jump itself was the 'Hero' content; it was a huge stunt that drew massive attention. That video has received 46.5 million views to date, driving people to the channel. Then Red Bull followed up with 'Hub' content: an engaging video that looked at 'the man behind the parachute', which was more documentary in style. Finally, they ticked the 'Help' box by having a video all about the stats related to the jump, so anyone who was searching for information about the height he jumped from, or how long it took to free-fall, would find their answers.

Playing this concept out for you as a brand, think about your objectives and see if any of these three categories would fit with your ambitions for the project. If you are looking to grow your YouTube or social media channels, to increase brand awareness for your product or increase website traffic, then 'Hero' content could be the way to go. Think about how you could create a 'tentpole moment' that shines a massive spotlight on your brand. Filming a PR stunt is a great place to start, and working with influencers is another good tactic for getting maximum eyeballs on your video.

I'll give you a great example of this. Burger King recently decided to take the preservatives out of its burgers. By doing this, it gained an edge over its competitor, McDonald's, simply by being able to make the claim that they are preservative free. Burger King decided to run a campaign[28] with a timelapse video of their burger going mouldy while the McDonald's burger stayed perfectly intact. The video they produced was surprising in every way– in fact, for many it was downright shocking. For me, personally, it put me off eating a fast-food burger in the immediate aftermath. Many people couldn't believe that Burger King would run an advertising campaign that made their burger look so unappetising. However, now that the dust has settled, I can't really remember the mouldy burger, but I can remember that McDonald's burgers are full of preservatives, so now I'm more enthusiastic about buying from Burger King, whose burgers are additive free. What clever marketing.

If your objective is authority building, increasing trust, positioning your brand in a particular light or just getting customers to fall in love with your brand, then 'Hub' content might be the right fit. You can begin populating YouTube, your social channels and your email marketing with entertaining or informative content that your customers get lots of value from. You need only look at TikTok to see how well people respond to entertaining content. Brands have turned their sights on using this platform to spread their branded messages around the hashtag #challenge. For example #cookiechallenge encourages users to try to stick an Oreo cookie to their head before trying to eat it with no hands.[29] This is a genius piece of marketing that provides endless entertainment, while not disrupting users' experience on the platform. The branded message is in there, but it isn't an advert.

Finally, if your objective is search engine optimisation, website traffic, lead generation or generally educating your customers better, then 'Help' content is a good place to start. Discover the questions your customers are asking and begin answering them with video. What information do they need from you to make their purchase decision a lot easier? Could you create a video to help with that?

For example, we worked with the investment platform Interactive Investor. They are the country's second largest direct-to-consumer investment platform and have a really user-friendly, informative site that makes it easy to invest in stocks and shares and other personal finance products. Their objective was clear: they wanted to drive more novice investors over to the platform and draw attention to their Stocks and Shares ISA and self-invested personal pension (SIPP) products. On Google, some common search queries are 'What is a stocks and shares ISA?' and 'What is a SIIP?' So we created two animations that answered these questions directly and a third one called 'Stocks and Shares ISA vs SIIP'. These videos now drive more traffic to Interactive Investor's website and have increased their search rankings on Google; they also help customers get quick, easy information about the different choices available.

By the way, if you want to watch a video of me talking about the different types of content on YouTube, head to **www.resonancebook.co.uk/videos**

Step 2: Look for ideas

As you know what type of content you are creating, you can now start looking around for ideas that will resonate with your audience. Remember that you only need the seed of an idea to get a project started. You can then rely on your team, partner agencies or video production company to help that seed germinate and grow into a fully fledged video production concept. Turn to your audience for inspiration and to steer you in the right direction.

What are your audience's interests?

Think about what your customers are 'into' that might give you some inspiration. If you sell life insurance to retirees, would their interests be cruises, gardening and Pilates? Is there any subject they find interesting that aligns with your product, like financial planning? Or perhaps you have a skin beauty range that's aimed at young adults. What do they do with their time when they are online? Maybe it's chatting with friends on Snapchat, creating videos for TikTok or shopping for clothes. You could just create videos with beauty and makeup tips, but you might discover that having bad skin is a major pain point for them and leads to low self-esteem and mental health issues. Could you create content around that topic that helps your customers?

If your brand sells cameras, I might be your target customer – photography is one of my passions. I'm a married 40-something father living in London. So what am I up to when I'm on the internet, and what are my other interests? I'm on YouTube looking at DIY videos for home improvements, so you might get to me there. I watch Gogglebox on Channel 4 on-demand, so advertisers reach me there. I shop for other gadgets on Google and Amazon. I research where we can go on holiday via sites like TripAdvisor and Lonely Planet. And I'm part of some Facebook groups about photography. See all these access points where you can reach me, and the potential content that might catch my attention? As a camera brand, it wouldn't fit to create DIY content, but you could run an advert to me about your product either on YouTube or during the Gogglebox ad break. However, the holiday research provides a better clue. For me, one exciting part about a holiday is getting the camera out and snapping some great pictures. So you could create content around that like 'Top 10 holiday destinations for the perfect shot' or 'The ultimate camera kit list for your holiday bag.' And clearly, if I'm on Facebook engaging in photography groups, then reaching me with relevant content about your products would be a great idea.

Where does your audience hang out?

As well as looking for inspiration in terms of your audience's interests, also think carefully about where they hang out. Baby Boomers aren't into social media as much as other generations, so you'd have a better chance of reaching them via Google and VOD. For Generation Xers like me, we use a bit of social media and YouTube and we dip into most platforms. Millennials are bigger social media adopters, so Facebook and Instagram are great places to reach them. For Generation Z, TikTok, Snapchat, Twitch and other younger-skewed platforms may be a better fit. It makes sense that you wouldn't create a load of TikTok videos if you were selling life insurance to retirees, in the same way that you wouldn't play an advert before *Loose Women* if you were trying to reach Generation Z (although students have sometimes been known to create cult followings around daytime shows). By deciding on the sorts of places you imagine your videos showing, you'll narrow your options when it comes to brainstorming ideas.

Think about all the potential places where your audience could view your videos and what state of mind they might be in at the time. Are they looking at the news on the *Independent* website or the *Daily Mail*? Or maybe they get all their news from Twitter? Are they looking for recipe ideas on *BBC Good Food* or a new fitness routine on *Men's Health*? Do they download games on their phone, and if so, what kind – Sudoku or Fortnite? Do they chat with friends via WhatsApp or Facebook Messenger? Are they posting on Instagram or LinkedIn? Do they have a subscription to Spotify, or do they listen to music for free on YouTube? Are they watching TV via streaming services on their smart devices or are they Netflix junkies? All these questions paint a picture of your customers' behaviour and provide options for reaching them, whether that's with adverts or branded content.

What's their path to purchase?

Keeping your customers' shoes firmly glued to your feet, think about the journey they take when they are looking for a product like yours. This should give you some great ideas for video content that can smooth the way for them and remove any barriers to buying from you. I'll go back to myself as the budding photography enthusiast. I'm looking for a new lens for my camera, so what do I do first? I look on YouTube for advice about the best lens. I literally type 'best lens for Canon 5D camera' and see what comes back. Once I've got the overview, I'll dig deeper into each brand by visiting their websites to compare one lens against another. Finally, I'll shop around for the best deals via third-party retailers like Amazon or Jessops. What could you do as a brand to help me on my path to purchase?

First of all, you could create videos ranking the top 10 Canon lenses, including those made by your competitors. Or maybe you could rank your own lenses or compare one against another. That will help with my initial search. Then you could add product videos to your website that list the features of each product and show them in action. That would make it easier for me to do my research without having to read too much text. Finally, after I've landed on your site and accepted your marketing cookies, you could remarket to me with display adverts on Google as I continue my buying journey.

Often the best place to start is on your own website – then work outwards from there. Take a look at your landing pages for customers who are finding out about your products. Could you create videos for those landing pages that provide instant, easy information? Is there a chance that your product is a bit tricky to understand? Do you need an explainer animation to unpack its key benefits? If you have a high-ticket item that's a hard sell, then maybe some customer testimonial videos or case study videos might help to prove it's worth the money? You might even have a common sales objection that your team encounter and this could be addressed with a video.

We've created a whole suite of website videos for dashcam brand Nextbase that takes customers on a journey from not knowing the brand to purchasing the product. Every time we come up with a new Idea for a video, it's designed for a specific purpose. We have YouTube videos showing real-world crashes from their dashcam to drive brand awareness; on the company's website, we have videos about the product, animations explaining the key features, and a video explaining how to install the product in your car;

and there are also some short product videos for Amazon and other third-party retailers to smooth the path to purchase.

Look at your competitors

You are competing for your customer's attention with other brands that do the same thing as you, so take a good look at what they are doing. What types of content are they creating and how are they using that to win sales away from your brand? Don't be derivative and just copy what they are doing. Come up with new ideas and original approaches that will make you stand out from your competitors' video content.

There may be some easy wins that you can identify. If you are a company offering life insurance, for example, have other companies created video content around the top reasons for choosing life insurance? You might find that when you look at your competitors, they all look very similar. Imagine what that's like for your customers as they are trying to research the right product. If all the suppliers look the same, it will be hard to choose. You might find that by creating a video about your company that's full of personality and even puts your team on camera, you might make your brand stand out.

Don't just look at direct competitors in your industry. Look at other similar industries that are also trying to capture your customer's attention. If you sell electric guitars, look at live music venues. If you are a car brand, look at holiday companies. If you are a museum, look at charities. If you are in banking, look at insurance. What types of content are they creating and how are they trying to reach their customers?

Step 3: Brainstorm

This is the exciting part: it's time to get the creative juices flowing. Whether you are going to work with your own team to come up with the ideas for video, or relying on an external agency, make sure you break out the whiteboard, dry markers and Post-its. Or use a bit of software if you find that easier. I find that **Miro.com** and **MindMeister.com** are both great ways of brainstorming ideas.

You're going to take everything you've discovered so far and come up with a game plan for the creative Idea. This is the part where you nail down your Idea. You know your objective and the outcome you want to achieve. You've got a great understanding of the types of content that could achieve your objective, and you've done your digging into your audience and what video content might resonate with them. Now you need to just go for it and let your imagination run wild. No Idea is a bad Idea, so encourage everyone to contribute – no matter how silly or banal they think their thoughts are.

Start by writing your objective, audience and outcomes at the top of the board. Then put your customer in the centre of the board with a circle around them. Draw lines out from the customer and start listing all the places you could engage with them – your website, social media, shopping sites, retailers and so on. Then start brainstorming ideas for content that could fit on those platforms. Think about the 'job' the video is doing for each customer access point. Is it explaining your product, advertising an offer, giving more detail, building trust? Is it 'hero' content to drive awareness, 'hub' content to engage your audience, 'help' content to make them find you and learn more, or are you 'advertising' to them?

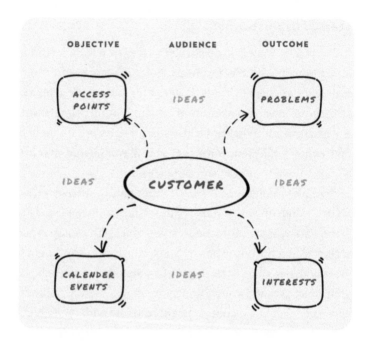

Think about dilemmas your customers face every day. Some may be mundane and common to most of us, like what clothes to wear in the morning, what lunch to eat, how to lose weight, how to find a partner, how to make more money. Others might be more nuanced to particular demographics, like 'where to go on my next luxury holiday', 'how to feed my family for £5' or 'what to do in my retirement'. For ideas with problems people experience, look no further than Google. You can use the keyword planner with Google AdWords to discover what answers people are searching for, and there are a few other great tools you can use like Answerthepublic.com. Even just typing into Google 'How do I [input activity]' and then scrolling down through the results until you find Google's 'People Also Asked' box will give you lots of other ideas and suggestions. In addition, *They Ask, You Answer* by Marcus Sheridan is a great book around this subject.

Look at upcoming calendar events that you could hinge your content around. Is your product perfect for chasing away the January blues or keeping my kids busy during the Easter holidays? Can it help me lose weight in time for my summer holidays or stop me putting it on around Christmas? From Veganuary to Movember, Halloween to Black Friday, our entire diary is packed full of opportunities for creative video ideas to leverage the current zeitgeist. Make sure you have all these calendar events in your diary so you can think about video content that would work for them.

Get all your ideas out and then start to assign titles to them. If you find a good title, it's more than likely that the video content will be a hit. Would *you* watch *The World's Biggest Knickerbocker Glory*, *10 Foods That Make You Thin*, *A Dashcam That Can Save Your Life*, or *Stock Market Investing In 1 Minute*?

Hopefully, your whiteboard is now packed full of ideas. Keep them all, because a good video content strategy comes from consistency and volume. You'll want to keep these in your back pocket for future campaigns. But for now, just pick your best ideas and start to flesh them out. We find that a simple one-page brief is enough to decide whether an Idea has legs or not. Interrogate every aspect of it to see if you think it will resonate with your audience and, if it does, then it's time to move to the next stage of the Resonance Method. We are going to inject Drama through the quality of our storytelling.

TOP TIPS

1. Don't pluck ideas out of thin air. Tie them to your Vision for the project.

2. Really research your audience and understand what makes them tick.

3. Create ideas for video around your customers' problems.

4. Provide value to your audience with videos that are entertaining, educational or informative.

5. Video works best when it does one thing well. Try not to muddle too many ideas together.

6. Think of ideas for videos that can help your customers at different stages of the buying process. Try to smooth their path to purchase.

7. Involve as many people as you can in the ideas process. Brainstorm different concepts and choose the best ones.

CONTINUE YOUR BRIEFING DOCUMENT

Fill out the next section of your briefing document, including your Idea in as much or as little detail as you want (if you haven't got yours yet, head over to: **www.resonancebook.co.uk/starterpack** and download it)

VIDEO PROJECT
BRIEFING DOCUMENT

PROJECT CONCEPT

Our Idea is to create a (*type of content*):

....

....

....

...to help our customer (*benefits to customer*):

....

....

....

We're titling this video (*name*):

....

....

OUR IDEA

Include a description of your Idea:

....

....

....

....

....

....

....

....

Visit **www.resonancebook.co.uk/starterpack**

for a digital version of this briefing document.

DRAMA

WHY DRAMA IS SO IMPORTANT WHEN IT COMES TO VIDEO STORYTELLING

We all need a little drama in our lives, wouldn't you say? Because life would be incredibly dull without a few highs and lows. It's the peaks and troughs of our daily lives that makes us human. All good stories are based around a bit of drama. Whether we are regaling our friends with a tale of winning £100 on a scratch card, getting soaked by a lorry driving through a big puddle, getting an unexpected pay rise at work or burning the Sunday roast, the stories we tell start with a moment that is dramatic, relatable and memorable.

If you want to create video content that resonates with your audience, you also need to think about how you can weave a bit of Drama into your production. If a great Idea is about grabbing your audience's attention, Drama is about holding it. It's about creating an engaging video that keeps your audience riveted to the end.

To get this right, you need to absolutely nail your storytelling and then make sure you tell that story in the most engaging way. It's about adding your own personality to your films, so they truly reflect your business and leave your audience feeling delighted that they've engaged with you.

Drama is really important when it comes to video storytelling; if you don't get that part right, it can lead to:

▶ A video that completely tanks even though adequate budget has been spent on all the other parts of the Resonance Method

▶ Your audience becoming bored with your story and stopping watching

▶ Your story becoming completely unrelatable so that no one engages with it

▶ Something unmemorable, so it doesn't leave a lasting impression and doesn't ever build any organic momentum

▶ You kicking yourself because you mucked up the simplest but most important part of your video project.

A common misconception is that the success of a video project is largely down to the creative ambition and the quality of the production work, and that all you need to

"

THE BIGGEST-BUDGET
PRODUCTIONS WILL
TANK UNLESS THE
STORY IS GOOD.

"

make your video successful is a massive budget. In reality, the biggest-budget productions will tank unless the story is good. We see it all the time with Hollywood blockbusters that rely on having a massive budget and the best visual effects, but they fail to have a good story and a well-written script. The result is that they flop at the box office. Ever heard of such mega productions as *The 13th Warrior* or *The Adventures of Pluto Nash*? No? I'm not surprised.

In the world of online video content, good Drama and great storytelling trump a high production budget every time. Video sharing platform Wistia conducted a fantastic experiment to test out this idea.[30] They created three online adverts for the same product ('Soapbox') at different budget points. The first production cost $1,000, the second $10,000 and the third $100,000. Inevitably, there was a huge difference in production quality between them, with the first one being made on a shoestring and the last one having premium actors, production staff and equipment.

Wistia then ran the adverts on Facebook, Instagram and YouTube to see which one got the best results. The data they gathered was incredible. Overall, the $100,000 advert performed the worst, with the highest cost per view of the three adverts. But what was most interesting was the $10,000 advert; it performed twice as well as either of the other adverts, with half the cost per video view, and they spent half the amount of advertising budget to acquire each new customer. So what happened?

When they looked at the different productions, they realised that the $1,000 and $10,000 budget productions hadn't been able to rely on just creating impact with their shots, actors and team, because they couldn't afford it. Instead, they had to focus much more on Drama and storytelling, injecting humour and authenticity through the script writing and cast of actors. The $10,000 budget production had the best script and really nailed the storytelling. This resonated far more with the audience and made it much more effective.

THE ANCIENT ART OF STORYTELLING

It was 2008, and I was making a TV documentary series about the Mafia for the National Geographic channel. I'd left my editor and edit suite in Soho, London to fly to San Francisco. To say I was nervous would be an understatement. What I was about to do was far outside my comfort zone. Not only that– it was borderline risky. Another director had recently quit the team after receiving a death threat from a Mafia member she was trying to interview. This wasn't a game. As I sat in my economy seat on the Boeing 747, at least I knew this would all be over in 24 hours and I'd be back on a flight to London. This was my big break as a TV director and it all hinged on the access I'd gained to the individual I was about to go and interview. The documentary was about the Italian Mafia in New York, and the person in question was called Alphonse 'The Professor' D'Arco. Not only had he been the acting head of the Lucchese crime family, but he was responsible for ordering multiple murders as well as committing a few himself. He was by all accounts a nasty piece of work.

For me, this had all started with a presentation I'd made three months earlier to the assembled members of the New York FBI's organised crime task force. That in itself had been a terrifying experience, but I'd somehow managed to convince them that bringing an 80-year-old mobster-turned-rat out of witness protection to give his first-ever TV interview was in the interests of the viewers of National Geographic. They had agreed, despite the threat to Al's life from many people involved in organised crime whose family members were now in prison due to his testimony. For the FBI, it had been the single largest takedown of organised crime in several decades and, frankly, they were keen to show off.

I arrived in San Francisco jet-lagged and nervous. I checked into my identikit hotel room and grabbed a few hours' rest while I waited for the call from my FBI contact, who would give me the time and place of the interview. The call came in, I collected my camera team and we arrived at the location in question, a nondescript, grey government building on an unremarkable street. I entered the room to discover the Professor waiting patiently for me.

He looked like a sweet old Italian man. Like someone's grandpa. Not the murdering criminal the FBI would have me believe. 'Hi, I'm Al. Nice to meet you,' he said, and I shook his leathery hand. After some niceties, he sat down, and we prepared for the interview. I'd come to interview Al about a particular part of his story that involved a series of murders in the 80s that were the feature of our documentary. However, Al wasn't going to settle for only filling me in on a small period of his life; he was ready to spill the beans. So when he started with 'It all began when I was 8 years old...' I knew I would be in this for the long haul.

I interviewed Al for four hours straight and I will never forget the vivid detail with which he brought his story to life. A natural storyteller, who talked about his favourite restaurant in the same breath as the time he shot someone to death in a bagel bakery. He flitted between sweet old man in whose mouth butter wouldn't melt and ruthless murderer, his eyes lighting up in fiery anger. It was the most compelling and unique interview I've ever done as a director. As I flew back to London with absolute gold on tape, I knew this documentary would be an amazing first foray into the world of directing. My boss would be chuffed to bits.

Stories. That's one of my most dramatic, and I hope it sparked your imagination. Alphonse D'Arco is a master storyteller whose life would be the basis of any good drama. I learnt my craft of storytelling through a career in the television industry and, bar none, it was always the most important part of creating Drama for any TV series. Without a well-told story, a programme was dead in the water. So learning to tell the story in the right way was a critical skill as a director. When it comes to creating video content for your brand, you need to inject Drama through your storytelling, as it's the single most important factor if you want to create resonance with your audience.

HUMANS ARE NATURAL STORYTELLERS

From the dawn of our existence, stories have been as much a part of our human DNA as any other aspect of life. The drama of our day-to-day lives is remembered and recounted through stories. Without them, our ancestors wouldn't have been able to hunt so effectively, form strong relationships for survival, or create bonds with one another to ensure lasting communities. In the earliest archaeological records of human habitation, where we see evidence of stone arrows and campfires, we also see cave art where prehistoric man and woman recorded their stories in permanence for future generations. It seems almost impossible to link the cave paintings of humans over 40,000 years ago to a set of emojis on Instagram today. But the reality is that human communication is constantly evolving.

It's easy to get distracted by the latest technology for telling your story, like video... or podcasts... or voice search... but just remember that the greatest storytellers throughout history didn't rely on gimmicks, tricks or the latest technology. The medium they used was just the vehicle for them to communicate their story and memorialise it in history. The story of Rameses II was written in hieroglyphs on an Egyptian pyramid wall, the ancient Greeks wrote on wax tablets, Jane Austen penned her novel *Pride and Prejudice* on paper,[31] and Steven Spielberg's *ET* remains a cult classic not because of the animatronics but because of the expert storytelling. Fads come and go – we're seeing that with recent hype surrounding the resurgence of 3D cinema and the second rise of virtual reality – but the principles of creating compelling content remain, and they've been the same since humans first started scribbling on cave walls.

As we find new ways to communicate, it drives us forward (for better or worse) as a species and leads us to leaps forward in our understanding of each other, the world and the cosmos. From cave art to the written word, from the printing press to telegram, telephone, radio, television and satellite communication, each of these technologies has created immeasurable advances in the human race. They have helped to create a hyper-connected planet where we no longer live in isolated populations with our own narrow understanding of the world around us. There has been no greater shift in human behaviour, knowledge and globalisation than with the advent of the internet.

Today, with smartphones, an individual can walk around with the knowledge of 100,000 years of human history in their pocket. They can instantly communicate with an individual on the other side of the planet in the blink of an eye. They can move and interact in communities of millions of people without leaving their bedroom. They can draw, write, print, play games, record radio, video, watch television and even do live broadcasts to millions of people on a device that sits in the palm of their hand. Never before in human history have we been so well connected and empowered by technology.

Some may consider the internet, smartphones and social media to be a negative influence on society. In fact, it can be easy to look at the world and blame the internet for the state of things. And why not? We have had a resurfacing of nationalism with Trump, Brexit and the far right manipulating mass communication to their own ends. Populist leaders are in power who are taking us backwards to misogyny and coal power. Kids today have their heads buried in smartphones rather than interacting in the 'real world'. Paedophile rings seem to operate unchecked, and terrorist groups use the internet as a platform for hate and destruction.

However, if you take a different perspective, the internet means we now have an ability to make real positive change to the world that would not have been possible before. The Arab Spring came as a direct result of people having access to smartphones and social media so they could communicate directly with each other and swap experiences. The #metoo movement has exposed a huge problem with sexual harassment in the entertainment business and has opened a conversation that is changing the way people understand feminism. During the Covid-19 crisis, video calls were a way to keep families and friends connected. For environmentalists trying to show us the truth about climate change, the internet and smartphones have been invaluable. The problems we are experiencing in today's society aren't new ones; they've been part of the human story for thousands of years. The internet just makes us see them in plain sight, but it's the internet and the technology that delivers it to us that I believe will ultimately save humanity from mutual destruction.

At this point you may be thinking, 'So that's all great and I take your point, but what the devil does this have to do with video?' Well, the reason I've taken you on a journey in storytelling from cave art to the present day is to make you understand the responsibility you have as a marketer when you start to craft your own Drama with video and communicate your story to the world. As a French revolutionary (or Uncle Ben to Peter Parker in *Spiderman* if that tickles your pickle) once wrote: 'with great power, comes great responsibility.'[32]

You have the power to influence people and to do great things in the world. With the reach that a piece of video content can now have, you need to consider what impact you want to have on your fellow human beings and what legacy you want to leave behind. A compelling story told through video can change millions of minds for better or worse. We need look no further than the Cambridge Analytica scandal for evidence of what a powerful advertising campaign can do to the world. Through deep data harvested illegally from Facebook users, coupled with up to 50,000 variations of advert[33] that had highly personalised messaging, this company was able to directly influence the outcome of the 2016 US presidential election.[34] Some people believe it was integral to Donald Trump's rise to the presidency. By all means, begin to tell your story with video– but you should do it with trepidation and excitement, because you are a change maker and already a part of human history.

HOW TO INJECT DRAMA INTO YOUR VIDEO

Step 1: Get clear on your story

After that beautiful tangent into the art of storytelling, let's get back on point. How can you actually harness Drama and storytelling for your brand's video? The individual stories you tell with video need to feed into your overarching brand story. Until you are clear about the story you are telling as a brand, it's going to be difficult to know what videos you can use to complement this. If you are crystal clear about your brand story, then congratulations – you've overcome one of the hardest hurdles in business and are ready to start telling individual stories with video. If you're unsure about your brand story, then don't worry – you are not alone. A huge proportion of brands don't spend enough time looking at this aspect of their business. I highly recommend reading Donald Miller's *Storybrand* for a more in-depth look at brand storytelling but, for now, let's go over some of the most important aspects to get you started.

What problem do you solve?

It seems obvious, but your brand is here to solve a problem. That problem is something your customers experience and need help with. At Small Films, we help marketers get their customers' attention with great video. At Ergonomic Desk Chairs, we stop people getting back pain at work. At Electric Motor Hire, we provide customers with cars that don't harm the environment.

We created some video content for an alcohol-free beer company called Lucky Saint. The brand story they tell is clear from the get-go. The founder was frustrated that there weren't any good non-alcoholic beers on the market. All the well-known breweries were creating strange concoctions of water flavoured with ingredients and additives that made it taste like beer. This leads to an artificial-tasting product. He found a way to create real beer in the traditional way and then just remove the alcohol. He solved the problem of there not being any delicious, alcohol-free beer for non-drinkers. The video we created was aimed at educating bar staff to communicate the quality of the product to their customers, helping them overcome the problem of what to drink on a night out when they can't have alcohol. What problem do you solve and how does it play out in the Drama of your customers' day-to-day lives?

Is your customer the hero?

Getting clear on the problem you solve is a good place to start, but in Donald Miller's book, he likes to use the 'Hero's Journey' as a framework for speaking to customers. This idea was first identified by psychologists and anthropologists before being popularised by literary professor Joseph Campbell in the middle of the 20th century. I love this framework as it's one which resonates with me and I use it all the time.

The hero's journey is a structure that most great stories fit into and is often considered the basis of all good dramas. And, if you ask me, it's also the perfect way to create resonance with a story's recipient. Many of the most successful books, plays and movies of all time follow the 'hero's journey' structure. Before them, many of the myths and legends told throughout history also followed this structure. When the hero's journey is missing, you inherently feel it – even if you don't know why. When it's missing, movies, books, TV series or brand stories often fall flat. The hero's journey taps into our inherent view of the world and our place within it. In fact, we go through our own hero's journey daily, monthly and through our lifetime.

The hero's journey focuses on a 'hero' whose world is disrupted. They go on a quest with the help of a guide, meet a villain and face adversity, but they overcome their fears to succeed in their task, and return to their regular life changed for the better. I'm going to use JRR Tolkien's *The Hobbit*, one of my favourite books from childhood, as an example. And it goes like this…

The story focuses on our hero (Bilbo Baggins). We open the story with this hero in his normal world (Hobbiton), where status quo is maintained (life is good and just the way he likes it). Then an event happens which was not expected (a load of dwarves turn up on his doorstep) and so the status quo is disrupted. The hero's life is upended (he finds out about a whole world beyond his own community), and he is faced with a dilemma – stay in his disrupted life or accept their quest and go on a journey of discovery and self-improvement (which would involve helping the dwarves recover their birthright while Bilbo discovers his own true calling). The way will be hard for the hero, and he will struggle to do it alone. Luckily, a guide appears to help him (the wizard Gandalf) and enables him to navigate all the pitfalls of the journey he goes on (travelling to the dragon's mountain). The hero meets a villain (the dragon), who he must overcome despite his fears and self-doubts. After twists and turns along the way, he discovers things about himself and the world and emerges victorious in the end (he tricks the dragon and recovers the treasure). The hero returns to his old life but now he is enlightened, changed and improved. He goes back to Hobbiton a hero.

So many stories you can think of follow this pattern and centre around a hero whose life is disrupted and then goes on a journey with the help of a guide – Luke Skywalker and Obi Wan Kenobi, Harry Potter and Dumbledore; even Bridget Jones navigates the pitfalls of her love life with help from her friends. The reason the hero's journey resonates with us so much is because we see ourselves as heroes in our own journey. We are constantly experiencing the hero's journey throughout our lives. It's those everyday moments of Drama that we go through all the time.

Our first foray into parenthood is the hero's journey incarnate. Life is simple, the status quo is maintained... then everything is turned on its head when we find out we are pregnant. We have no choice but to go on a journey into parenthood with help from our own parents, friends, midwives and self-help books to adapt to the new normal. We also go through the hero's journey when we change jobs, move house, experience trauma or suffer loss. It's those obstacles that are thrown in our way throughout life that we must overcome if we are to keep going.

So, where does the brand story fit with this principle of the hero's journey? It's quite simple, actually. Your audience is the Hero. You, as a brand, are the Guide. Paying attention? You are the *guide*. You are not the hero. If you can remember this one thing, it will serve you well with all the stories you tell. Make sure you avoid falling into the trap of creating a video that's a giant ego-stroking exercise for the company. Your job is to help your customers navigate the pitfalls of life and go through their hero's journey with the help of your product or service. If you are a credit card company, your job is to guide your customers to overcome the problems of personal finance. If you are a golf club brand, you guide your hero through the challenge of nailing the perfect swing. If you are a coffee producer, you must guide your hero through life's twists and turns with a reassuring and comforting cup of coffee.

When you tell stories as a brand through video (or indeed any other form of communication), you must cast your customers as the hero and tell a story they will relate to, with your product as the guide. That's what will create resonance and help you connect with your customers on a more meaningful level.

What's your brand purpose?

Your brand story isn't just about the problems you solve for your customers and how you can help them; it's also about the overall image you are projecting of your organisation. It's the big picture for your customers when they ask themselves, 'What is this brand all about and why should I care?' Your brand story is your opportunity to communicate your purpose and mission as a brand. This has never been more important than it is today, when 75%

of millennials say they care about the purpose of a brand.[35] The days of faceless corporations who just make money are gone. Every brand nowadays needs to tie itself to some form of purpose and corporate responsibility. Follow this link to watch a video I recorded about this topic:

www.resonancebook.co.uk/videos

How you tell that story is absolutely critical. Consumers can smell bullsh*t from a mile away, so things like 'greenwashing', where a brand runs an environmentally friendly campaign purely for publicity purposes, won't work. Your brand purpose has to be authentic and real. It has to align with your whole brand story and make sense for people.

Tilda Rice is committed to helping end world hunger and so it partners with the World Food Programme on charitable initiatives. Tilda asked us to produce a video which told the story of their collaboration with this charity and a programme to deliver nutritious meals to starving mothers and their children in developing countries. The story they were telling was genuine and real, and the company can prove this by having donated 5.8 million meals to mothers in need. We decided to create an animation using photographs of women who were benefiting from this scheme. We also made a point of starting the film by focusing on the subject of childhood malnutrition and the risks to development. We established the story and created resonance with the viewer before introducing the brand message and the call to action (buy a specially marked pack of rice and Tilda will donate a nutritious meal).

Think about your own brand and what could be important to you. A good place to start is to align your organisation to the UN's Sustainable Development Goals. This gives a great starting point to discover your purpose. At Small Films we are aligned to the global goals of Climate Action, Life on Land and Life below Water. As film-makers, we are passionate about capturing the world around us on film, and so seeing the effects of humans on our environment is something we care deeply about. It's also something we can help with directly, through our side projects and the content we create; a portion of all our invoiced work goes towards various charitable causes that align to these goals. What are your passions and how could you help the wider community as a brand?

Step 2: Create individual stories with video

Now we've looked at the overarching brand story, let's talk about the individual stories you can tell with video content. What stories will help to paint a bigger picture about your brand? Go back to the Vision for your campaign and the Idea you've settled on. We talked about creating content around your customers' problems, but there are other stories you can tell with content that won't have to revolve around problem solving.

What story will you tell?

The simplest is the story that you tell about your product. Sometimes, people just need to know that your product exists and that it can help them. If I'm a parent looking to buy my child a birthday present, then a quick advert on Facebook about the latest microscooter might be the perfect story to resonate with me. If I see a child of a similar age to mine having fun riding a scooter, it will connect with me in that moment.

Another story might be about an initiative you are running, like a partnership, a charitable act or a particular scheme. For example, we created some content for nut milk brand Plenish that showed vegan recipes as part of the Veganuary movement they were partnered with. That told a story about veganism and how you could take part.

The individual stories you tell could be about an aspect of your business that people don't know about, like your recruitment policy or that you are carbon neutral. It could be to do with your supply chain, a new product development or the celebration of an important milestone.

Remember your audience

Don't forget that you are trying to tell a story that will resonate with your audience, so remind yourself who you are speaking to.

In practice, ensuring you are clear about your audience can be the difference between success and failure. We were commissioned by Eton College to help them with a very specific challenge. Every year, they award £1m in fully paid bursary places to bright boys from underprivileged backgrounds whose families can't afford the fees. These boys could come and study at Eton with all fees and expenses covered by the school– but every year, Eton failed to attract enough applicants and so those places were left empty. They wanted to see whether creating films about the initiative could help.

For us, this was a clear objective and had a very specific audience. We knew that any content we created needed to strike a balance: showing off the history, tradition, facilities and opportunities that Eton represented without looking unapproachable to state-school-educated candidates who might not be able to relate to it. By following one boy – Joshua, who grew up on an estate in Camberwell, South London – and showing him playing basketball with his mates back home and then playing football with friends at Eton, we could tell a relatable story that resonated with the right audience. As a result of the project and a lot of press attention, Eton was oversubscribed for their next open day and all those places could be assigned to boys who deserved them.

Have you distilled your message?

When you tell your story with a video, you need to be clear on your message. Whether you are creating a six-second advert, one-minute Instagram post or two-minute website film, you will quickly realise that video is a medium that benefits from having a simple, concise message. I often say to people that writing a script for a two-minute company film is one of the best exercises in getting clear on what you do and the value you bring. When you can't rely on an entire website of text and images to tell your story, you are forced to strip out absolutely everything that is non-essential and only focus on the most important parts.

Don't make the mistake of trying to cram as much information as you can into your video. Save that for your other communication. Video is about teasing your customers, saving them time, giving them a snapshot and welcoming them into your world. Unless it's an e-course or webinar, then a video needs to be kept simple and free from information overload. If you try to include too much information, you will find that your message gets diluted and the viewer doesn't retain the relevant information.

List three main points

Start by listing three things your video needs to communicate. This is a great place to start and will give your story the right structure. Typical things you may want to communicate are who you are, what you do, who it's for, the problems you solve and the next steps for customers to take. However, this will be nuanced to your individual brand and your individual story.

For example, we created a series of 10-second adverts for the Scottish ice-cream brand Mackies that formed part of a summer campaign. In 10 seconds, you really can't squeeze much more than three thoughts in. In this case, the three points were 'real dairy ice-cream', 'made with fresh milk and cream', and 'making simple delicious'.

With the longer videos that fully explain your product, you will be able to include more information – but try to ensure that information feeds into the three points you want your customers to go away with.

We created a company video for StreetDots, a digital platform that connects street food vendors with landlords who have outdoor space to rent. For them, the three points to communicate were that 'they are a new bit of technology', 'they solve the problem of landlords with unused commercial space and vendors who can't find pitches for their street food vans' and 'the platform is easy to use'. The stories we crafted all fed into these three points and informed the voiceover script we wrote and the shots we filmed.

When you are clear on the three points you want to communicate, it will help you to craft a compelling narrative and create a video that hits all the right tones of a good Drama. If you are relying on a third-party supplier to do this part for you, then it will make their life a lot easier.

Step 3: Inject some Drama

Have you split your story into three parts?

The best stories are simple, relatable, engaging and memorable, and a lot of that is down to how you actually craft your narrative and the mechanics of storytelling. So let's start with the structure of a good story. It seems obvious, but when you tell a story, it must take the listener on a journey. It can't just be 'A man walked into a pub. The end'. There needs to be a beginning, a middle and an end – known as the 'narrative arc' or 'three-act structure'. Look at most plays, movies and novels and you will usually find they follow this principle.

This idea of dividing a story into three acts taps into the very nature of human oral tradition. Think about a time recently when a friend has told you a story about something that happened and I can guarantee that, if it was a good story and memorable, they had automatically broken it into a three-act structure.

As an example, let me share this story with you. Act 1: 'Did I ever tell you the story of how I met my wife? I was walking to work about three years ago. I'd just picked up a flat white and was crossing the road when this cyclist comes out of nowhere.' Act 2: 'She collided with me and knocked me over. I got absolutely covered in coffee. I was sprawled on the floor, but as I got my senses back, I looked up and realised she was the most beautiful woman I'd ever seen.' Act 3: 'I was completely struck by her and asked her to marry me right there on the spot. She laughed and said, "No thanks." However, we swapped numbers and, after a date or two, we were madly in love. Six months later, she accepted my proposal, and we were married.'

Do you see how this little story broke down into three acts, with a beginning, middle and end? Also, notice how this story is simple, in that it has a single narrative thread, it's relatable because it could happen to anyone, and it's engaging because of the very nature of what happened – something that is not an everyday, mundane occurrence. It's also emotive: it makes the listener feel dismay when the coffee is spilled and elation when the couple connect. It follows a structure that makes it engaging. All those things combined make it memorable, and so it's easy for the listener to retell to others. Much more interesting than the real story, in fact, which was that I met my wife at the office Christmas party, the end. (There is a bit more to my story than that, and I absolutely love her to bits.)

The three-act structure is an incredibly important aspect of good storytelling and applies to online video content as much as any other form of communication. Sometimes, the content might only last six seconds– as in the case of a YouTube advert, for example– yet that three-act structure still applies. In a piece of content this short, six seconds may only equate to six individual shots, so storytelling becomes even more important.

For example, imagine you are a brand selling paint to consumers wanting to redecorate their homes. The whole USP of your brand is that it only takes one coat of paint to transform a room. You know your audience consists of time-poor homeowners who can afford the premium that your brand commands, so you set the scene with a young, affluent couple in their new home. They open a door to reveal a ghastly room with lime-green paint flaking from the walls. That's Act 1, and it took one and a half seconds. Act 2 sees them open the can of paint and start painting. The clock on the wall shows 1pm. That shot took just two seconds. Act 3 sees the room completely finished and looking beautiful. The couple stand back with their arms around each other. The wall clock shows 2pm. The message on screen reads 'One Coat. One hour. Job done.' Act 3 concludes our story in just two and a half seconds.

When you craft your narrative, think about it like a piece of music. It should have a natural flow. If you find that the story seems to be a list of 'And then... And then... And then...', as if you are moving from one point to another in a monotonal list without a rhythm, build and crescendo, then your narrative probably isn't very engaging.

Who will tell your story?

Once you're clear on your brand story and the individual stories you want to tell with video, and you've crafted a clear story arc, it's time to decide 'who' will tell your story to the viewer. This is your opportunity to inject some personality to the film and bring some added 'oomph' to the table so your videos truly titillate your audience.

Most of us have a friend or colleague who is a natural storyteller. Even more clearly, if you've ever been to watch a stand-up comedian, you'll know that timing, energy and body language all help to bring a great story alive. The same goes for telling a story with video. 'How' you tell the story is as important as the story itself.

Whether you are using your own staff, actors, voice-over artists, imagery or motion graphics, all these elements are an intrinsic part of bringing your story to life, so they need to do it in the right way. For example, if your CEO is a charismatic person who thrives on talking on stage, they'll probably do a great job of telling your story on camera; whereas if they are monosyllabic and low-energy, they won't do it justice. A skilled voiceover artist who resonates with your audience can inject lots of Drama into a script where an overenthusiastic narrator might be a turn-off. And a great actor can make your videos highly memorable where an amateur might make your product look amateurish.

With many videos, you may rely purely on imagery, motion graphics, animation or text to tell the story, dispensing entirely with spoken words. If this is the case, then it's all the more important to bring your story to life in an exciting and engagingly visual way that will be easy for your audience to follow.

Don't feel overwhelmed by the decisions about who will tell your story, as your video supplier or creative agency will help with this process. Just think about the personality of your company and the audience you are speaking to. What would reflect your brand in the right way but also resonate with your audience?

TOP TIPS

1. Reflect your overall brand story in the video stories you tell.

2. Keep your story simple. Don't overload it with too much information.

3. Think about your audience and the story that will resonate with them.

4. Avoid using insider language that might confuse your audience.

5. Create a clear narrative arc with a beginning, middle and end.

6. Make your customer the hero in your story, with your brand as their guide.

7. Inject some drama through your choice of storyteller. Avoid the monotonal staff member or overenthusiastic voiceover artist.

CONTINUE YOUR BRIEFING DOCUMENT

Fill in the next section of your briefing document.

VIDEO PROJECT
BRIEFING DOCUMENT

ABOUT OUR BRAND

Include a description of your brand and what you stand for:

....

....

....

STORY

Here are the three key points we need to deliver (*include the three key points*):

....

....

....

ADDITIONAL INFORMATION

Include any additional information you want to communicate with your video:

....

....

....

Visit **www.resonancebook.co.uk/starterpack**
for a digital version of this briefing document.

EXECUTION

WHY YOUR EXECUTION NEEDS TO BE ON POINT IF YOU WANT TO CREATE IMPACT

You are now well on your way to creating resonance with your customers through your video content. By creating a clear Vision for your video project with an understanding of your objectives, audience and outcomes, you should have been able to come up with a great Idea and inject some Drama through great storytelling. The next part of the Resonance Method is about creating impact through the Execution of that video. To do that, you need to produce your video content to the highest standard for the budget available. And that's done in two ways. The first is to ensure you have produced your best creative work,

REMEMBER, AN ONLINE AUDIENCE IS A TOUGH CROWD.

and the second is to ensure that the technical Execution is flawless. Whether you are creating this video with in-house resources and shooting it on an iPhone, or working with an external supplier using the latest camera equipment, now is the time to take your seed of an Idea and let it germinate.

But before we dive into the nitty-gritty, I want to share why the Execution is so important. Remember, an online audience is a tough crowd. We're all running around our busy lives with lots of better things to do than watch some branded videos. If the quality of your Execution is poor, a few things are likely to happen:

- ▶ Low-quality work will leave your customers with a negative impression of your brand; they will see you as amateurish or not caring about your brand image.

- ▶ Your videos will just get lost in the noise and receive poor engagement because they don't stand out from all the other average-quality work out there.

- ▶ The wrong technical Execution can lead to videos not being fit for purpose, so you then won't be able to use them in your Outreach.

- ▶ Your customers may feel like you've 'interrupted' their online viewing experience with poor-quality content. This can annoy them.

- ▶ Frankly, there's nothing worse than reviewing the finished video with the rest of your company and getting a poor reaction because the quality isn't up to scratch.

During the Covid-19 pandemic, the world's largest brands were trying to strike the right tone with their advertising, wanting to talk about themselves while also sympathising with the crisis we were all experiencing. So many of them tried to 'play it safe' that a lot of their adverts were almost identical. They were so similar in style that the internet started making fun of them.

Most started with '[cue slow sombre music] Here at [insert brand], we've been helping you [insert use for product] for [insert number of years] and we're here for you now through these troubled times.' They then go on to cue some uplifting music, say how they are looking to the future, and then show a montage of people looking happy and emerging from the crisis.

By playing it safe rather than thinking outside the box and not pushing the boundaries creatively, all these brands ended up with vanilla content that not only delivered very little impact, but also created bad PR for them and could even affect public opinion of their handling of the pandemic. Forbes even wrote an entire article about how derivative and unimaginative the adverts were.[36] It's a huge shame when brands don't get this right, because when you nail the Execution of your videos, you can get phenomenal results and drive huge attention for your brand.

CASE STUDY

CREATING THE FIRST EVER
OXFORD/CAMBRIDGE 'VIRTUAL' BOAT RACE

As a result of the Covid-19 pandemic, for the first time since World War Two, the famous Oxford and Cambridge boat race had to be cancelled. Advertising agency MCH London approached us to see if we could create a 'virtual boat race' where teams competed against each other from their own homes. We were excited to be involved and helped them to take the seed of an idea and cultivate it into a fully developed concept.

The Vision for this project was to raise awareness for Power2Inspire, a charity that promotes inclusivity within sports. The Idea was simple; the first Oxford and Cambridge virtual boat race, featuring both disabled and able-bodied rowers.

But what really made this video exciting and delivered impact was the Execution. First, we worked out the logistics of 'how' two teams could compete against each other from their own homes using just their rowing machines and their smartphone cameras. We coached each team member in how to film the footage themselves to get the best results for our film. We then mixed this home-filmed footage with high-quality animation that showed the boat race's usual course on the Thames. The whole thing was brought together by two BBC sports commentators who guided us through the race.

We injected Drama by creating build-up to the race, introducing the team members so that viewers felt invested in the race, and then creating excitement and energy through dramatic commentary. A PR agency then promoted the video with Outreach to the press and this led to phenomenal results.

The results were:

▶ 500,000 video views

▶ 20 pieces of national news coverage, including *The Times*, *Evening Standard*, BBC radio and the BBC Sport website

▶ Potential reach of 700 million people

▶ Direct fundraising for the charity more than doubled expectations

▶ Shortlisted for several awards including the UK Content Awards.

Watch the video here:
www.vimeo.com/428472744

Or scan this QR code:

HOW TO ENSURE THE PERFECT EXECUTION

Step 1: Choose your creative approach

It's important to have a general understanding of the creative approach you are looking for, as this will inform the type of video supplier you choose – for instance, whether you find an animation specialist or a live filming specialist. It's also going to help you turn your Idea into a well-developed concept and ensure your entire team are on the same page with the creative Vision for the project.

So where do you start? Because, let's be honest, unless you're a video nerd like me, you've probably had better things to do than geeking out on the best creative video work. Well, it's actually easier than you'd think.

First and foremost, the creative approach needs to resonate with your audience, but it also needs to reflect your brand in the right way. So, if you are a prestigious art gallery, an elegant creative approach using film might not only resonate with your audience but also reflect your brand; whereas, if you're a disruptive smartphone app helping Gen-Z to buy and sell vintage clothing, a loud and frenetic approach with motion graphics might work better.

Now head over to YouTube, Facebook, Instagram and any other channel you can think of to hunt around for videos by other brands that are selling to your customers – these brands might be in your sector or completely different sectors. The important part is that they are trying to get the attention of the same audience as you. If you find something you like, save the link to it.

For further inspiration, put your customers' shoes on and think about the places where they might be watching other online videos. These might be websites they would visit for celebrity gossip, lifestyle and wellbeing articles, or news. Look at the sorts of videos being shown to them and if you see anything that you think could work for your own brand, note it down.

What style did you see most? Were the videos serious or did they use humour? Were they informative or entertaining? Disruptive or educational? Did they use live filming or animation? Stock footage or user-generated content, like Zoom recordings and iPhone footage? Or did they have a mix of styles? Did they have actors or people drawn from real-life situations? Voiceover or text on screen? Were they shot out on the street or in a studio? And how was the product featured? Even think about the sort of music you thought worked well, and whether they used sound effects. There isn't one creative approach that is better than another. They all have their own merits. This is about choosing the approach that you think will work best.

Start collecting all the examples you've found and put together a kind of 'video mood board'. I've included an example of this that you can download with our video starter kit at **www.resonancebook.co.uk/starterpack** Create a one-page document with links to the examples you like, as well as some screen shots for a visual representation of the look and feel of the videos. If you can, add in a few music tracks that you think could work for your video. This will help your supplier understand the type of energy you are expecting from the film.

Try your best not to be derivative. If you see one video that you absolutely love, don't just try to replicate it. Come up with your own Vision and your own original concept. The number of times I've had brands ask if we can create a video just like the 'Dollar Shave Club video'... If you haven't seen this, it's a hilarious piece of content featuring the founder of the Dollar Shave Club in the USA. He capers around their warehouse delivering a funny diatribe about the merits of their product. The video went viral and put the brand on the map; it's largely credited with their business reaching a $1bn valuation within five years.[37] This led to numerous brands trying to replicate the style of the Dollar Shave Club video, desperate for a bit of that kind of success to rub off on them. Very few (if any) managed to create anything that came close to the original. Instead, they just look like copycats, which isn't great for anyone's brand. So find *your* voice, think about what *your* customers want, then settle on a creative approach that you think will resonate with them.

The different styles of video content

LIVE ACTION FILMING

This is a catch-all term for filmed video content. It might be a glossy advert with actors on set or it might be a simple vlog. It could be a two-minute product video or a five-hour e-learning course.

ANIMATION

Even though there may be no filming involved, animation requires just as much work. An animation could use characters to tell the story, or a mix of dynamic text and imagery. Animations can be in two dimensions or three dimensions and in a variety of styles.

COMPUTER-GENERATED IMAGERY

CGI is great for creating hyper-realistic footage of your products. Car brands often find that a CGI version of their car looks better than a filmed one, because rain, dirt and sunlight can play havoc in a live filming shoot.

USER-GENERATED CONTENT

Popularised and heavily relied upon during the pandemic, 'user-generated content' refers to anything that was filmed in a non-professional way. Footage from iPhones and Zoom recordings and other home-made footage can sometimes be leveraged to create compelling videos.

LIVE STREAMING

Many social media platforms now offer live filming, and it's a great way to drive a lot of attention for your brand. Often, going 'live' is a good way to drive awareness and engagement as part of a wider campaign.

360° VIDEO

360° videos are filmed using specialist cameras that capture a 360° perspective. When hosted on particular platforms like Facebook, the viewer can then interact with the video and drag their mouse to 'look around'.

MIXED MEDIA

Sometimes, combining different media can be the best way to create some compelling video content. Some elements might be filmed, some might have motion graphics or animation, and stock footage or CGI might get used.

INTERACTIVE VIDEO

Interactive video allows users to interact with their screen. On a basic level, this can apply to any piece of content with a level of interactivity; for example, you could click a button on a YouTube video and watch another video or visit a website. Other platforms allow lead capture and other calls to action. But on a more complex level, interactive video can be integrated into a company website and allow far more user interaction, including clicking on parts of the screen to open up more information.

AUGMENTED REALITY

As a simplistic description, AR is where users can look through their smartphone camera or through technology like Google Glass and see additional information overlaid onto their screen. For example, a user might look through their smartphone screen at a wine bottle, and an animation would 'magically' appear on the label.

VIRTUAL REALITY

Virtual reality has come on in leaps and bounds in recent years. The quality of the footage has improved exponentially and enabled really immersive experiences. You can allow the user to interact with the video content they are viewing and experience your stories in a whole new way.

Step 2: Define your technical specifications

Boring, I know! But defining your technical specifications is an absolute must if you want your video project to deliver the best outcome and to come in on budget. This is particularly important when it comes to hiring an external supplier. Suppliers charge for the work involved to create multiple versions of your video – for example, if you wanted a long version for your website and a short one for your social media. If you don't include this specification in your briefing document, you will get different quotes back from your suppliers and will find it hard to compare them. This could lead to a nasty surprise halfway through the project when you request a short version of your video for social media and are hit with an unexpected bill.

My point is that different versions, different aspect ratios, video length and what goes into the video from a technical perspective all affect the amount of work to be completed and also the cost. So you need to be clear with your 'tech specs' so your project costs don't mushroom out of control.

Now you're probably thinking, 'How the hell am I meant to know the technical specifications for videos? That's the video producer's job, isn't it?' And you have a point. But really, you just need to give a top-level overview based on what you think you'll need. Look at the Vision for the project and the Idea you cooked up. That should give you a good steer on the videos you're looking for. Tech specs can be changed through the course of the project, particularly as you get expert advice, but make sure all the suppliers are quoting on a level playing field so that it's easier for you to evaluate the quotes.

Things to think about

DELIVERABLES

'Deliverables' are the final videos that you want to produce. Do you need one video or multiple videos? Is it for your website or your social channels? Get clear on how many videos you are trying to create.

VERSIONS

You can often create multiple versions of the same video. You might want one for your website and a shorter one for your social media. Maybe you want to re-version your video for slightly different audiences, including different information or calls to action.

LENGTH

A video can be literally any length. GIF-style videos can be just a few seconds long, while Hulu broke the Guinness World Record for longest live video stream in 2019 when their team watched back-to-back *Game of Thrones* episodes and broadcast it for 161 hours![38] The length of your video is dependent on the platforms you are using and the purpose of the video. However, in the world of online video, a good rule of thumb is to 'make it short' – and, once you've done that, then 'make it shorter'. Very few promotional videos can go beyond two minutes before losing people's attention.

CALL TO ACTION

What do you want your audience to 'do' once they have watched your video? Is it 'Find out more' or 'Buy Now'? 'Follow Us' or 'Visit our Website'? Browse the 'Summer Sale' or take advantage of '50% Off?' Make sure you are clear on your call to action and give your customers clear instructions about what they have to do next. Customers want to know what to do next – so help them!

SOUND

General good practice in the online space is to design all your videos so they can work with the sound off. This is because a large proportion of people may not be using headphones or speakers when they watch your videos. In fact, 85% of Facebook users watch with the sound off.[39] So that gives you a clue to people's viewing habits. This may mean using motion graphics or subtitles to communicate the story if they can't hear dialogue. There are exceptions to this rule if you have a more captive audience; for example, TikTok users will have the sound on,[40] and if someone is engaged with your brand and looking for information on your website, they may be happier to engage with the audio.

ASPECT RATIO

Video comes in all shapes and sizes. The conventional aspect ratio is landscape (also known as horizontal, 16:9, or widescreen). But you can also create videos that are square (also known as 1×1), portrait (also known as vertical or 9:16) and a range of other shapes. Before smartphones, we only ever filmed things in landscape. That's how cameras shoot film and it's how our eyes view the world – but we hold our smartphones upright in a vertical position, which lends itself better to portrait videos. There are benefits to all the different aspect ratios, and they fit specifically with different platforms. It's important to get advice on this so you shoot the right type of content, because sometimes it's just not possible to retrofit one shape to another. So, if the video creator shot the entire video in horizontal aspect ratio for YouTube and you then ask for a vertical version for Instagram stories, you're going to encounter some major issues. Your objective is to make your videos fit natively into the platforms where they will be shown, so make sure you look at the current trends on those platforms and replicate them.

BRANDING

Your videos need to be on-brand and consistent with the rest of your marketing communications. Assemble your brand guidelines to share with the video producer. Make sure the fonts being used are correct, the company logo is the latest one, and the right colour schemes are being used. It's also worth gathering any other assets that the video producers may find useful, such as screen grabs of your social media feeds and YouTube channel, so the content you create reflects the pre-existing style you follow online.

REVISIONS

A quick one to mention here. Most suppliers will offer one or two rounds of revisions when it comes to the editing of your video project. If you require more (perhaps because of multiple stakeholders or intermediaries), you must stipulate this. More revisions will incur additional cost.

Getting as clear as you can with your technical specifications will help you with your next task of finding a supplier, while arming you with the right information to get the most competitive quotes.

Step 3: Choose a supplier

Because you are now clear on the creative approach for your video and on the technical specifications, it's going to be a lot easier to find suppliers and gather competitive quotes. At the risk of making a potentially self-interested statement, you get what you pay for when it comes to video content creators. Really think about the outcome you defined right at the beginning. If you are a business that's looking to drive £100m in sales, then you need to be hiring the best if you want to get there. If you have a very low budget and more modest expectations, then working with a junior videographer might be the better fit.

It's really important to understand the budget you are working with when you go to find suppliers. If you know what you are spending, then you can find the right fit. We always ask prospective new clients to give us a budget range to help us understand their expectations. Is this a £0–5K job? £5–10K? £10–20K? £20K+? Talking about money is an awkward conversation and I understand why marketers want to keep their cards close to their chest when it comes to budget. They might be worried that by revealing their budget, the supplier will take advantage of them, or it will prevent them from getting the best price – but let me share a quick anecdote about why being upfront about your budget is important.

A friend of mine runs a fantastic consultancy business. He wanted an animation for his homepage that summed up his business in a nutshell, and he asked if we would be able to do it for him. Knowing his business, I said that our fees would be inappropriate for the outcome that he would be hoping to get from the video; he had a small business with a modest marketing budget and I would not advise him to spend too big a chunk of that on creating a video with us. Instead, I offered to evaluate suppliers when the quotes came in. His marketing manager put together a solid brief to share with suppliers, but wasn't clear on their budget. They gathered five quotes: the most affordable was £1,500, and the most expensive was £18,400. The reason they varied so much was that each company was producing to a different standard. The £1,500 company was a young founder who was just getting started, while the £18,400 company had pedigree and worked with huge brands.

In reality, my friend had a sub-£5K budget, so only two of the quotes fitted in his budget range. So, from five quotes gathered, only two were relevant, and that's never a good way to make a decision about a supplier. On this occasion, he got lucky and was happy with the video his supplier delivered, but it doesn't always work out that way.

Even if you are going to produce this video project using an in-house team, it's still important to share the budget with them. That way, they will know what resources they can bring to bear on the project.

> *If you want to know more about how much a video costs, visit:*
>
> **WWW.SMALLFILMS.COM/HOW-MUCH-DOES-VIDEO-PRODUCTION-COST/**

Create your brief

Before you start looking at video suppliers, make sure you have a one-page brief that sums up your project. Include all the information we've been working on so far. The brief should contain your objective, audience and desired outcome, as well as your ideas for your video. Include your video mood board with examples of the videos you like. You'll also include as much information as you can about how you are going to tell your story, how many videos you need and for what channels. Try to include your budget within this briefing document, even if it's only a general ballpark figure or a range, as well as key dates for gathering quotes, the deadline for final delivery of the project, and any other key dates. This will set the expectation for the work. By having all the information, including your intended use of the video and the deliverables, you will be able to gather comparative quotes.

Look for suppliers

Look for video production companies that are the right fit for your project. Think about what's important to you. Is having someone local to your area important, or are you happy to work with countrywide or global suppliers? If budget is a major concern, you may need to work with a freelancer rather than a video agency. Or do you have a healthy budget and want a more specialist video creator? In that case, find out whether they have experience in your particular sector or experience of creating the types of videos you want to create. Have they worked with clients like you before? Look at their case studies to see if they fit with your ambitions for the project. Look at testimonials from past clients to see if they did a good job.

Request proposals

Ask potential suppliers to submit a proposal with examples of relevant work and a breakdown of how they will approach the project. Ask them to provide a quote detailing what will be included in the work, including team size, camera equipment, crew members and any other relevant information. What expenses are included and which ones are not included? If the first supplier's quote includes something that the second supplier's doesn't, then ask the second supplier what they would charge for it. For example, one quote might include voiceover fees, while another charges them separately. Or one might include travel expenses where another doesn't. You need to ensure that all your quotes have the exact same scope of work, so you can compare apples with apples.

Some suppliers may be willing to provide creative ideas as part of the pitch process; others may consider this to be part of the work that should be paid for. Some projects would benefit from an in-person presentation, while others can be decided by a simple one-page quote. As part of one large tender process, in the final stage of the competition, we actually had to create videos for the brand to show them what we could do. The suppliers had to invest in the pitch process to win it. This was what clinched it for us and led to us winning a six-figure contract. Asking the production companies to do all that work would not have been a reasonable request if the contract had been smaller.

Make a decision

Make sure you've had phone calls and meetings with your potential suppliers, because trust and chemistry are sometimes as important as experience and skill. You're going to be working with them for the next few months, so you want to know that you can rely on them, that they will work hard for you and that the entire process will be easy and fun.

Of course, you need to weigh up all the factors when making a decision about the supplier, but my one piece of advice is to not just pick one based on price. I know people who hired the cheapest option and had to reshoot the entire video because of technical problems, and others who hired the most expensive company and ended up with lacklustre results. If you have a question around a supplier's capability or prices, or another hang-up, then ask them about it. Arm yourself with as much information as possible so you can make an informed decision.

I've included a handy checklist for hiring a video supplier that is part of our video starter kit at:

www.resonancebook.co.uk/starterpack

Remember, I did say that to create the most impact through your Execution, you need to produce the video to the highest standard for the budget available. I always say 'for the budget' available because we all have different budgets for our videos. If you were a high-end fashion brand, you might not think anything of spending £50,000 on a video and photoshoot on a Caribbean beach – but for a fashion start-up, this would be prohibitive, and finding even £5,000 might be a struggle. Just remember: however you choose to produce your video, cut your cloth to the budget available. If funds are tight, don't try to be too ambitious with the creative. Keep it simple. And if you are on a shoestring and shooting this on an iPhone, then lean into that medium and be honest about the technology you are using. Sometimes the 'raw' feeling of using an iPhone can have impact in its own right.

TOP TIPS

1. Make sure you define your budget before seeking quotes from suppliers.

2. Create an accurate and thorough briefing document.

3. Check your video supplier's credentials. Ask for case studies and testimonials.

4. Don't just choose the cheapest quote. Inexperienced video production professionals can lead to shoddy work.

5. Try to find an original style for your video rather than copycatting other people's work.

6. Make sure your videos are formatted correctly for the intended platforms, like social media and YouTube.

7. Push your own boundaries creatively. No one ever won awards for playing it safe.

CONTINUE YOUR BRIEFING DOCUMENT

VIDEO PROJECT
BRIEFING DOCUMENT

STYLE
Our brand personality is (*description*):

....

....

....

Please find examples of our style here (*website, social links or images*):

....

....

....

INSPIRATION
We like the style of these videos (*include links to examples*):

....

....

....

....

We are interested in these elements for our video (*actors, voiceover, animation, music, etc*):

....

....

MOOD BOARD

We have gathered some imagery and video that reflects the direction of this project (*include the mood board*):

....

....

....

DELIVERABLES

- We need........(*number of videos*) in........(*aspect ratio*)
- Estimated length.......(*length of videos*) for.......(*platforms*)
- Our call to action is...

Note: Try to be as specific as you can with the exact number of videos you need.

VERSIONS

We need / do not need versions for other platforms:

....

....

Note: Try to be specific with whether you need different versions of your video for different platforms, like You-Tube, Facebook, Instagram Stories.

ROUNDS OF AMENDS

We will require.........(*include number of revisions*) rounds of revisions at the edit stage.

Note: Most suppliers provide two rounds of revisions as standard. Sometimes you may need more.

BUDGET

Our budget range is .... (*include a range*)

KEY DATES

Quotes to be delivered by....................................(*date*)

Supplier chosen by...(*date*)

Deadline for final project delivery is....................(*date*)

Other key dates include....................................(*dates*)

For a digital version of this briefing
document, head over to:

www.resonancebook.co.uk/starterpack

THE THREE STAGES OF THE VIDEO PRODUCTION PROCESS

At this point, you will have found a supplier and will actually start making your video. So it would be remiss of me if I didn't give you a brief overview of what to expect. It's important to understand this process so you can have more informed conversations with the video producer. In the video production world, we divide projects into three parts: pre-production, production and post-production.

Pre-production

This is the part of your video project that takes place before anyone picks up a camera. Initially, this will take the form of discussions between you and your suppliers. You'll nail down the creative approach and milestones for the project. During this initial phase, scripts will be written, storyboards created and shot lists prepared. All preparations will be made for the filming, including booking locations and crew, auditioning actors, buying props, hiring equipment, obtaining filming permits, arranging travel and logistics, and doing risk assessments. This part can take several weeks, or even months, to organise.

Production

This is the filming production part of the project, where the team actually shoots the video. In the online video world, filming usually takes one or two days but can be longer. Depending on the ambition of the project, the filming might involve a one-man band doing everything or a huge crew with dozens of people. Filming could take place in a studio, out on location or in both settings. It might involve complicated lighting setups, actors and set design, or it might just be a simple interview in an office somewhere. Production teams work very hard, so don't be surprised when 'call time' is very early in the morning and the shoot runs on into the night.

Post-production

Once the footage is captured, it then needs to be edited. The post-production process is where an editor will cut together all the footage into a compelling video. Editors usually report to a producer or director, who will work with them to craft a narrative and get the video working well before it's shown to you, the client. In this part of the process, motion graphics and visual effects may get added, as well as voiceover, music and sound design. The footage is also colour graded, meaning the colours are balanced and the footage is 'touched up' where possible. Usually you will be offered at least one round of revisions where you can make your notes and ask for changes. If you have commissioned an animation, then production follows a similar pattern but instead of filming anything, you may have WIPs (work in progress) shared with you at various stages of the process, including character designs, animation tests and rough edits.

CHAPTER 9

OUTREACH

CREATING YOUR VIDEO ISN'T ENOUGH – YOU ALSO NEED PEOPLE TO SEE IT.

Congratulations! By now you have created your video. By following the Resonance Method, you had a clear Vision, narrowing in on your objectives, audience and outcomes. You found the perfect Idea that will grab your audience's attention. You injected Drama through expert storytelling and created impact with the perfect Execution. You've created an epic video that resonates perfectly with your customers. Everyone is chuffed to bits with the finished video and the moment has come to 'go live' and put it out into the world.

It's important that you don't just throw your video up on your website, YouTube or social channels and hope for the best. You need a proper strategy in place for making the most of your films. And that's where Outreach – the final stage of the Resonance Method – comes in. Whether you've created an advert or branded content, whether it's a story about your company, your product or your customers, form a plan to put that content out there for people to see. Too often, marketers invest all their time and energy in creating the video content and don't spend any time in promoting it. But that's like building a rocket and not putting any fuel in it. Videos rarely just 'go viral'. No matter how good the content, it will need a boost to make it visible for people.

If you don't plan your Outreach and work hard to put your video in front of your audience, it's likely that:

▶ The project will end up being a giant waste of time because none of your customers will actually see your video

▶ You will get low views, poor engagement and very little traction

▶ You won't deliver on the objectives and outcomes you set at the start of the project

▶ Because you can't demonstrate success, you won't be trusted to do further projects, and budgets will be withheld from you

▶ Not only will the team be left demoralised, but your own reputation will suffer.

On the other hand, when a solid strategy for Outreach is in place, you can get incredible results. Dove ran a campaign called 'The Campaign for Real Beauty', hoping to ignite a global conversation about the definition of real beauty. It centred around 'Dove Real Beauty Sketches', a three-minute YouTube film looking at how women view themselves. It was a wonderful piece of video content built from an amazing Idea that was Executed flawlessly. But Dove knew they needed a solid plan for Outreach if they wanted it to gain momentum. They ran paid advertising on YouTube and focused heavily on a PR launch when the campaign was released. This gave the video the initial boost it needed. Media and bloggers picked up on the campaign, leading to an estimated 4.6 billion impressions and 163 million video views globally,[41] making it one of the highest viewed online adverts of its time. The vast majority of that visibility was completely organic, but none of it would have been possible without Dove initially paying for some degree of Outreach.

HOW TO ENSURE YOUR VIDEOS HAVE REACH

Step 1: Amplify your videos

Now is the time to put all that hard work into action. Put your videos out there and do the hard work of amplifying them as loudly and for as long as you can to get maximum reach. Invest time, energy and, where possible, budget in your Outreach and amplifying the power of your video content. Even the best branded content ideas, with a great concept and excellent execution, can benefit from having paid advertising behind them.

With mobile video, you have the ability to reach your customers wherever they are, 24/7. Ask yourself if you have explored all the potential options for increasing the reach of your video and whether there are any other platforms you could leverage effectively. Here's a quick overview of some of the most likely places where your customers could see your videos.

Brand or product website

Websites are always a great place to start. Your customers will be looking to buy and are researching your business. Don't just provide them with a single website video – consider unpacking your story with multiple videos as they move through your site.

Social media channels

For customers who follow you on social media, you can serve them regular, useful content through your own pages. Facebook, Instagram, Twitter, LinkedIn, Pinterest, Snapchat, TikTok, Reddit, Twitch – all of them have the option to use video, and there are new social platforms appearing all the time. As for customers who don't follow you on social media, you can reach them through paid advertising.

Popular websites

Think about your customers' interests and the websites they visit frequently. Most of these sites offer an opportunity to reach your customers with video. There are news sites, magazines, blogs, networking, education and learning sites, shopping sites, directories, maps and many others. You can either advertise to your customers through display adverts on those sites or sponsor your own content; for example, a sponsored article on a news platform or a sponsored recipe video on a cooking blog. Even music streaming sites like Spotify now run video adverts, so don't underestimate the numerous opportunities to reach your customers.

Apps

Most of us have dozens of apps on our smart devices to do everything from playing games to organising our to-do list. Apps that are free to download will serve adverts to users as a way to cover the cost of the installation. As marketers, it's very easy to serve adverts through apps. Look no further than the Google Ads platform to do this. When you run display adverts through Google's Display Network, many of your adverts will be shown on popular apps.

Messenger services

Many of us now use direct messenger services to talk to our friends, from WhatsApp to Facebook Messenger. In fact, many of the social media platforms' direct message functions act as another way for us to communicate with family and friends. Apps like WhatsApp don't currently allow advertising, but you can still use the platform as an informal way to reach customers. For example, tour companies will sometimes set up WhatsApp groups for their guests, which then offers an opportunity to follow up later with promotions. Social media messenger services are free for the user, but users have to agree to receive promotions from advertisers.

Email

If your customers are subscribed to your newsletter, email is a superb vehicle for sending out your video content. And if you are prospecting for new customers, including video is a good way to increase open rates and engagement. We even include videos in our email footer for regular communications.

There are a few ways you can use video in an email. The simplest way is to embed it using your email provider, like MailChimp or HubSpot. The user will see a thumbnail of the video with a 'play' button. When they click it, it takes them to the video on your homepage or YouTube channel. You can also get the video to play directly in an email, if you shrink the file size down to a few megabytes (so it doesn't fill up their inbox). If you want to get more sophisticated, you can create a GIF which plays on loop automatically, or you can actually code video into your emails using HTML.

Point of sale

Consider where your customers are actually buying your products. Do you sell direct from your website or through third-party retailers, like Amazon or another well-known shop? By creating videos explaining your product, you can help your customers make better purchase decisions. Consider actually advertising to them on these websites; if they are on the site, it's likely their purchase intent is very high.

Search engines

YouTube is one of the best places to increase the reach of your videos. You can either advertise to customers using the platform or create videos that answer the questions they are searching for. Google is also another great option. When people enter a search query, Google doesn't just return search results in text form – it also includes videos. Put your video on your product or blog pages to boost SEO. Amazon is also used by customers as a search engine to research products, so consider advertising on this platform if you sell there.

Out of home

Moving from online to offline, out-of-home advertising can work hand in hand with your online content. Increasingly we're seeing more and more digital billboards when we are out and about, from the big screens of Piccadilly Circus to smaller ones on the front of vending machines. It's often a simple move to take your online content and rework it for out-of-home advertising. Consider all the places your customers could see your content when they are out of the home, such as the cinema, in-flight movies, taxi cabs or in-store displays.

Online television channels

VOD (Video On Demand) use has skyrocketed in recent years, with all the major TV networks now offering online access to their content. But despite being able to pick and choose what shows and movies we want to watch, we are still subjected to advertising. It's how the networks make the money they need to create the TV programmes. This now offers a fantastic opportunity to reach your audience. You can show your customers adverts or even sponsor a TV show that aligns with your brand.

Influencers

Influencers sometimes get a bad rap. But remember that not all of them are famous solely for being famous; many have skills and passions that could align with your products. People turn to their favourite influencers for all kinds of life advice, from fashion tips to cooking, fitness to mental wellness. Influencers inspire their audience and can provide aspirational role models for the next generation. By including influencers in your video projects, you can increase the video's reach in a major way.

The mail

I've saved this one for last because I'm less keen on this option– it's not great for the environment. However, you can actually send your video to people via the mail. There are companies that can produce video brochures for you that are nicely designed and include small screens that will play your video. Alternatively, you can send out a memory stick in an attractive box. If you have a very small, laser-sighted audience of people who are otherwise impossible to reach, this could be a great fit. We once worked with an entrepreneur whose target market was senior leaders in the pharmaceutical industry. She sent out a small number of video brochures to these people and immediately grabbed their attention.

From the start of this project, you should have had a plan for what versions of the video you were creating, but now is the time to really interrogate whether you have some more options for video reach. To begin with, consider your plans for the video shoot. Is there a way to create more assets from that shoot than you had originally intended?

For example, if you are creating a two-minute film about your brand and you will be featuring your products, could you also get some additional footage of those products and create some social media content from it? Could you get some behind-the-scenes footage of the shoot and put that on social media? Think about all the ways you could take the footage that's shot on the day and create more videos from it.

Also think about the video you are creating. Could you create a long version and a short version? Could you create a version with a small enough file size that you could embed it in an email? Could you create some GIFs (moving images) from some of the footage? What about the aspect ratio? Would it work to have a 16:9 horizontal version for YouTube and a 1×1 square version for Facebook? Are there other ways you could promote the video itself across other channels? For example, could you do a Facebook Live promoting the video launch? Or release a series of simple, self-shot iPhone videos on Instagram to create buzz around your main video? What about creating a blog about the video that attracts even more website traffic to it?

All the different versions of your video will help to create an ecosystem of content that drives your viewers from one place to another. You can serve them a 10-second advert on Facebook that drives them to your website landing page video. Or you could wait for someone to watch the video on your landing page and then remarket to them with shorter versions via Google display advertising.

With all our clients, we try to get the maximum value out of a single shoot, filming as much material as we can to create as many video assets as possible so they can be used in lots of different places. In some cases, we might even translate the videos into multiple languages for multiple territories. Really put some thought into all the ways you could amplify your video content and make your message as loud as possible.

Understanding your customers' viewing behaviour

Being creative with your video content isn't the only thing that will create impact and grab your customers' attention. It's also about creating the right type of video content that will resonate with your audience at the right time, in the right place. Think about how your customers will be viewing your video content. Are they more likely to be on desktop or mobile? Websites or social media? Take a look at Google Analytics, where you can get information about the traffic to your website. And think about your access points, like websites, social media or apps.

Currently mobile accounts for around half of all internet traffic globally,[42] and the vast majority of that use is to access social media. We're spending around 145 minutes per day scrolling through our social feeds.[43] It's a statistic that blows my mind, but it's not one that surprises me.

"

ALL THE DIFFERENT
VERSIONS OF YOUR VIDEO
WILL HELP TO CREATE
AN ECOSYSTEM OF
CONTENT THAT DRIVES
YOUR VIEWERS FROM ONE
PLACE TO ANOTHER.

"

When we check our phones, it tickles the pleasure sensors of the brain, releasing dopamine, which makes us feel good; it's the exact same action that happens when we smoke cigarettes or take recreational drugs. But just like cigarettes and drugs, when this behaviour becomes habitual, it also becomes addictive. Every time we compulsively check our phones for text messages, social media updates or even just our fix of the news, we are trying to top up those dopamine levels, even if it is to the detriment of our personal lives. In the UK, the average person checks their smartphone every 12 minutes[44] and in 2020 we clocked a massive 2 hours and 19 minutes a day on our smartphones. Over 10 years, that's nearly an entire year (352 days) of our life spent looking at a tiny screen![45]

We know that 83% of all social media use happens on smartphones.[46] However, even that number can be subdivided depending on which social media platform people are using. SnapChat, for example, is a mobile-only social platform. Until recently (April 2020), TikTok accounts couldn't even be accessed via desktop. And while Facebook sees 81% of its users access the platform via smartphone,[47] for LinkedIn that figure is just 57%.[48] So already you can see that different audiences exhibit different behaviours. LinkedIn, while a social platform, is inherently tied to work and business, so it's perfectly acceptable to scroll through your feed at your desk in the office. In stark contrast, most offices won't tolerate their employees browsing Facebook when they are supposed to be working.

People's viewing behaviour changes depending on how they are accessing your video and what state of mind they are in at the time. For example, a bored person scrolling LinkedIn via their work PC at 4pm on a Tuesday may be more likely to watch a two-minute video than the same person scrolling Twitter at 9am on a Monday as they travel into work. Equally, someone lying in bed at 10am on a Sunday will happily indulge in a 15-minute YouTube video, but they wouldn't be in the right state of mind to watch the same video in the dentist's waiting room.

Facebook have a very particular way of describing how users interact with content on the platform that says a lot about people's viewing behaviour. If you want to know more, then I've recorded a video about it that you can watch here: **www.resonancebook.co.uk/videos**

Step 2: Build your infrastructure

When you put the right infrastructure in place, it will enable you to leverage your videos effectively. For example, if your video is part of an advertising campaign that is driving people to a landing page, make sure the landing page is designed and ready. If you are planning to run a Facebook campaign, build your audience within Facebook and get your advertising copy ready. If you are going to host your videos on YouTube, make sure your channel is set up and ready. If you are working with an external video production company or other creative agency, they should be able to get all these elements ready for you. If you are handling this in-house, then make sure you have someone who is dedicated to this, as it can be quite time consuming. Building this infrastructure is not that complicated, but it will involve coordinating the different people who will be helping to get this together.

Where will you host it?

Where will you host your video? There are a range of different video hosting platforms, including Vimeo, Wistia and of course YouTube. Or you may want to host the videos directly on your social channels. Consider the purpose of your video and how it's being used. That will help inform the platform you choose. Typically speaking, we recommend Vimeo, because you can embed a video on your website and remove all the Vimeo branding so it looks professional. However, Wistia and other platforms offer other unique benefits like user interactivity.

If SEO is a major consideration, you may want to use YouTube; embedding your YouTube video on your site will help improve your rankings for Google searches. Unfortunately, the video will be covered in YouTube branding, which can make it look quite unprofessional. If you do decide to use YouTube, make sure your YouTube channel is optimised with the right colour palette, branding and consistent 'thumbnails' for each video. Organise your videos into playlists and make sure you've added things like end cards and tags.

If you are uploading your content to your social media channels, make sure you upload them natively (directly to the channel) rather than embedding a You-

Tube or Vimeo link. Videos that are uploaded natively to social channels will play automatically for viewers, whereas embedded videos need to be clicked on. For more information about using video on YouTube and your social channels, read the guide I've included in our video starter kit: **www.resonancebook.co.uk/video-starter-kit**

What's the best posting schedule?

Whether you are posting a single video or a series of videos, make sure you and your team are clear on the schedule for going live with these videos. Depending on video length, file size and internet speeds, a video could take an hour or more to upload to the web– so if you are planning, say, a 1pm launch, allow plenty of time to get your video uploaded. If you aren't sure how long it will take, or how this will work, then for Pete's sake practise it and do a dry run! If you are planning a daily, weekly or monthly release of videos, make sure you have created a content calendar with a to-do list and assigned tasks for team members. Make sure everyone knows which platforms are being used, which versions of the videos fit with those platforms, the hashtags you will be using, and what time the videos need to go up. Put all this into a document so it's easy for anyone to take on this task.

Are you ready to run a glitch-free digital ad campaign?

If you are planning on boosting your video content through paid advertising, make sure you have built out the infrastructure for this campaign. Whatever platform you are using, and whether you are doing it yourself or working with an external agency, this will take time and energy to set up. It might seem obvious, but you do need to make sure your account is active, that the payment cards are set up correctly, and that you've got pixels on your website so that platforms like Google or Facebook can give you data about the success of the campaign. You need to have done audience research within these platforms and segmented the different audiences that you are going to advertise to. You should also make sure you have the right advertising copy to complement your videos, and that this doesn't repeat what you are already saying in the video itself.

If you are using a media buying agency, programmatic advertising or a third-party tool, make sure you've allowed plenty of time for the groundwork to be done on setting up your campaign. There may be very specific technical specifications for your videos that will be communicated to you. In particular, videos can take time to be 'approved' by the moderators of these platforms and be given the green light to go live.

When you set up your campaign, it may also throw up questions over the videos you are creating and whether they are the right length or format for their final use. By being prepared with your digital advertising infrastructure, you'll be able to fine-tune your videos ahead of the launch.

We worked with a UK boarding school that was looking to attract overseas students. We created a series of videos about the school for the purpose of advertising on Facebook and Instagram. These then directed the audience back to the school's website, where a two-minute video of the school's boarding facilities would play. We managed to get a large volume of traffic to the site, but visitors encountered a stumbling block when they couldn't easily find a way to download the school's brochure. Once the school redesigned the landing page and made this process easier, it led to the advertising campaign being successful. This illustrates how the video itself is just part of the equation; you also have to be set up to leverage it effectively and drive the desired outcome.

The entire digital advertising ecosystem is now highly automated and very advanced in how you can reach customers. If you are new to this, then I'd recommend starting with mastering Google Ads and Facebook Ads. Both these platforms offer a tremendous amount of potential reach and are relatively easy to use. With the Google Ads platform, you can not only run the standard text-based ads, but you can also use the Google Display Network to show video advertising on websites, apps and other platforms. You can also create YouTube advertising campaigns directly from this platform. With the Facebook Ad platform, you can create campaigns on both Facebook and Instagram, two social networks that have a phenomenal number of users.

Step 3: Measure

When you make your videos 'live' and put them out for the world to see, you'll need to make sure that you measure their performance. This step is a crucial round-up to your video campaign and will help you to demonstrate the success of your video project. By gathering data, you will be able to provide evidence to other stakeholders that this video really worked.

Look at the KPIs you laid down when you were getting clear on your Vision for the project. Have you hit them?

Did you increase website traffic as much as you had hoped? And have you improved your search engine rankings? If your priority was customer acquisition, then how have you performed against your goals? Or if increasing sales was the focus, did you deliver on your objective?

Look back at all the metrics I listed in the chapter on Vision and see if there are any other ways you can measure the success of your project, from press mentions and awards to video views, likes and shares or social media growth. Could you gather together a few testimonials from customers, or even your team members, where they react to the video?

Build as comprehensive a picture as you can of the success of this project and gather it all together into a post-match analysis report that you can share with your team. It will be this evidence that will enable you to unlock further budget and make video an integral part of your marketing plan.

Having success in this field is not just about having a single win; it's about consistently putting out video content and optimising what you are doing. Remember that the Resonance Method is about giving your videos the best chance of success – but sometimes, you will do everything right and the videos still don't perform as well as you'd like. Looking back, you might realise you didn't quite nail one aspect of your project, so the video didn't resonate with your target audience. Other times, your video will be a viral hit but when you compile your report, you can't put a finger on why. The hard truth is that the more content you put out, the more likely it is that you will have a runaway success.

TOP TIPS

1. Create a plan for Outreach at the very beginning of your video project.

2. Make sure to allocate enough time and resources to Outreach.

3. Research your audience and the best channels to reach them.

4. Don't spread yourself too thin across too many different channels.

5. Get your digital marketing infrastructure in place with plenty of time before you want your video to go 'live'.

6. Create different versions of your video for different digital marketing channels.

7. Make sure you do a report on the successes of your video campaign, checking results against the outcomes you defined at the start of the project.

COMPLETE YOUR BRIEFING DOCUMENT

Fill out the final part of your briefing document and you will be ready to go!

VIDEO PROJECT BRIEFING DOCUMENT

OUR PLAN FOR DISTRIBUTION

We plan to increase the reach of our videos in the following ways *(List ways)*:

....

....

....

....

OTHER NOTES

Include any other notes you think may help the supplier to provide an accurate quote:

....

....

....

....

RESULTS

Fill this out once your video project has been completed and you've measured the impact. Link it to the outcomes you defined at the beginning:

BRINGING IT ALL TOGETHER

Around of applause to you, reader, for embarking on this journey to unlock your brand's potential with video. You really are one of the very few who have chosen to take their video marketing know-how to the next level. Just by reading this book, you've given yourself a massive advantage over your peers. By following my simple five-step process, you can begin to create real resonance with your customers through your video content. When you create that moment of resonance, it's going to be a game changer. You just wait and see. The moment you create a video that flies, you'll be chomping at the bit to do more and more. And the more video you create, the better results you'll get, and the bigger your brand can grow.

QUICK RECAP

Remember that it starts with having Vision. Don't just embark on a video project in a haphazard way without a plan. Get clear on your objectives, audience and outcomes. That will inform your entire video campaign. Use that Vision to come up with a good Idea. This will give your audience a damn good reason to view your video. Take that Idea and develop it further, injecting Drama through your storytelling with a simple, relatable and engaging message that resonates with your audience. Make sure the Execution of your video is performed to the highest quality for the budget available, then amplify its effect through a well-considered plan for Outreach.

CREATE YOUR BRIEFING DOCUMENT AND GET TO WORK

If you've been completing the exercises I've been sharing with you, then you should now have a completed briefing document. If you skipped that part but are now ready to get started with your video project, go back over the five-step process and populate your briefing document now. (Download via this link: **www.resonancebook.co.uk/ starterpack**)

Once you've filled out this briefing document, use it to get all stakeholders aligned on the ambition you have for your video campaign, and to get the work started with your supplier. This will also serve as a reminder for the direction of the project as you progress, so you don't get steered off course.

THAT PERFECT MOMENT OF ABSOLUTE RESONANCE

I always stress-test the Resonance Method when we create our own video content, but I also look at other brands that have created video campaigns which have resonated so deeply with their customers that they have runaway success. I look at those campaigns and I see whether the rules of the Resonance Method apply. I want to share one with you now, because this is the kind of project you could be doing for your brand right now.

In 2016, food brand Knorr released a video called *Love at First Taste*. I'd be surprised if you didn't know Knorr, because they are in virtually every supermarket and have been going for years. Their main product is stock cubes, and I always remember them from the adverts on TV: 'Knorr... They've got the K-now how'. This is quite a traditional brand whose image was associated with that antiquated view of Mum in the kitchen, cooking for the family. Their vision was to change that. They wanted to start appealing to a younger, Millennial crowd and to revitalise their stuffy image. Their objective and audience were clear, and the outcome they wanted was 1 billion earned impressions.

Next, they needed a good Idea. So they did their homework; they looked at their audience and searched for common traits that linked them together. They realised that Millennials are united by their often single status and participation in internet dating through Tinder and other platforms. So Knorr explored that as an idea. They surveyed 12,000 millennials in 12 countries and found that 78% of them said they'd be more attracted to a partner if they enjoyed the same flavours of food.[49] One in three claimed they would be worried about the compatibility of a long-term partner if they didn't like the same flavours. And that was the basis for their idea.

They created a 'Flavour Profiler' quiz on their website that people could fill out, and the results put each respondent into a 'Flavour Profile' category. Knorr then ran a social experiment, matching people based on their flavour profile. They created their three-minute film *Love at First Taste* featuring couples on first dates, brought together through their love of food.

To ensure this film had the most impact, they wanted the Execution to be flawless, so they hired a top creative agency which, in turn, hired a director who had won awards for a similar short film called *First Kiss*. They threw the best team at it and had the budget to have high production quality. They then injected Drama through expert storytelling and creativity. And finally, they had an incredible plan for Outreach, including the use of multiple videos that supported the main campaign.

The showpiece video was on YouTube, but Facebook was used to drive sharing and Twitter for conversation. People who completed the Flavour Profiler quiz were sent bespoke recipe videos for their flavour profile. Knorr did partnerships with video content platforms like Tastemade, and also used influencers and social media advertising. The results were unreal. The campaign created so much buzz that they got around 1.6 billion 'earned' impressions, worth around £10m.[50] They estimated the impact of the campaign to be three times what could have been accomplished with the same paid advertising budget.

The film was the second most viewed YouTube ad that year, with 54 million views. Among a list of other metrics for brand uplift and sales, Knorr increased their brand appeal by 7.6% and their global market share by 1.4% as a result of this campaign.[50] This film resonated on a deep level with their target audience and gathered incredible momentum to propel the brand into the spotlight. Bravo, Knorr.

GO FORTH AND CREATE

If you haven't created online content for your brand, then get out there and start doing it. If you are already creating content but want to take it to the next level, start thinking about your audience and what will resonate with them. Remember, we're all exposed to so many commercial messages every day that it's hard to grab your customers' attention. But when you create content that resonates with people, you can increase love for your brand and become the brand everyone is talking about.

If you are intimidated to begin your first video project, I understand, but don't be worried about failing. We learn from our mistakes – and for every flop you have, you will be getting closer to a winning video. The more you create, the better chance you have of success. Being prolific beats being perfect every time when it comes to video content.

I believe that brands can make a positive impact on the world with their content and I'm on a mission to show people how to do that. When you start to think of yourself as a publisher and begin creating content that adds value to people's lives, not only can you create impact for your brand, but you can also have a positive impact on people's lives and on the wider world. We have plenty of low-quality, pointless content that's adding to the noise in the online space. It's up to you to go out there and start making a difference with content that has a purpose and a reason for being there; content that enriches our world and changes lives for the better.

When you start creating content, yes, you'll win awards. Yes, you'll drive sales and increase customer engagement with your business. And yes, you'll get prestige for your organisation and great feedback from customers. But it's so much more than that. Brands that create fantastic content can build a tribe of loyal followers who start to see that business as more than just the product it sells. Nike, Red Bull and Patagonia represent more than just shoes, an energy drink or a clothing brand. They've become ingrained in popular culture and their content is a must-have destination for their audience.

So what are you waiting for? Go forth and create. Become a content creator and gain the power to change the world. I get that you might be nervous. I get that it seems daunting. But if you need any help getting started on this journey, why not reach out to my team and me so we can help? We've worked with all sorts of brands, from those first dipping their toe into the video world to others who've had failed campaigns and need help to master the medium. The Resonance Method we go through has worked with them and it can work for you too. And if you decide to go on this journey yourself, I want to hear from you. Let me know about your successes.

Email me at **george.hughes@smallfilms.com**

PS: Did you spot the secret ingredient that leads to the greatest chance of your videos going viral?

ENDNOTES

1 https://en.wikipedia.org/wiki/Hot_or_Not

2 https://www.prnewswire.com/news-releases/facebook-reports-fourth-quarter-and-full-year-2019-results-300995616.html

3 https://www.businessinsider.com/generation-z

4 https://www.ofcom.org.uk/__data/assets/pdf_file/0024/149253/online-nation-summary.pdf

5 https://www.ofcom.org.uk/about-ofcom/latest/features-and-news/decade-of-digital-dependency

6 https://nypost.com/2017/11/08/americans-check-their-phones-80-times-a-day-study/

7 https://www.statista.com/topics/7425/digital-advertising-in-the-uk/

8 https://www.ofcom.org.uk/about-ofcom/latest/media/media-releases/2020/uk-internet-use-surges

9 https://toomanyadapters.com/tech-questions-inca-trail

10 https://www.marketingweek.com/intelligent-technology-future-marketing/

11 https://whatsnewinpublishing.com/investment-in-online-ads-to-account-for-51-of-global-total-key-highlights-for-publishers-from-warcs-latest-report/

12 https://always.com/en-us/about-us/our-epic-battle-like-a-girl /

13 https://www.campaignlive.co.uk/article/case-study-always-like-a-girl/1366870

14 https://www.statista.com/statistics/216573/worldwide-market-share-of-search-engines/

15 https://www.forbes.com/sites/forbesagencycouncil/2017/10/30/the-value-of-search-results-rankings/#2675b90e44d3

16 https://www.statista.com/topics/2019/youtube/

17 https://www.statista.com/statistics/284506/united-kingdom-social-network-penetration/

18 https://nytimes.com/2007/01/15/business/media/15everywhere.html

19 https://www.forbes.com/sites/forbesagencycouncil/2017/08/25/
finding-brand-success-in-the-digital-world/?sh=48bab46d626e
20 https://www.statista.com/statistics/874736/ad-blocker-us-
age-in-united-kingdom/
21 https://www.vox.com/recode/2021/6/24/22548700/google-cook-
ies-ban-delay-floc-tracking
22 https://www.businessofapps.com/ads/ad-fraud/research/
ad-fraud-statistics/
23 https://www.manchestereveningnews.co.uk/business/busi-
ness-news/swizzels-factory-features-bbc-twos-11788000
24 https://www.statista.com/statistics/286526/coca-cola-advertis-
ing-spending-worldwide/
25 https://en.wikipedia.org/wiki/Drugs_Inc
26 https://en.wikipedia.org/wiki/Dope_(TV_series)
27 https://en.wikipedia.org/wiki/Red_Bull_Stratos
28 https://www.independent.co.uk/life-style/burger-king-moudly-
whopper-ad-watch-a9344761.html
29 https://www.tiktok.com/tag/oreochallenge?lang=en
30 https://wistia.com/learn/show-news/introducing-one-ten-one-hun-
dred
31 https://www.themorgan.org/blog/jane-austens-writing-techni-
cal-perspective
32 https://en.wikipedia.org/wiki/With_great_power_comes_great_
responsibility
33 https://www.forbes.com/sites/forbescommunication-
scouncil/2018/05/01/what-the-cambridge-analytica-scan-
dal-means-for-the-future-of-facebook-marketing/?sh=18f5a897291c
34 https://www.theguardian.com/technology/2018/mar/19/face-
book-political-ads-social-media-history-online-democracy
35 http://workplaceintelligence.com/millennial-consumer-study/
36 https://www.forbes.com/sites/avidan/2020/04/19/every-covid-19-
commercial-is-exactly-the-same
37 https://www.inc.com/magazine/201707/lindsay-blakely/how-i-did-
it-michael-dubin-dollar-shave-club.html